SCHOLASTIC

JUNE
Monthly Idea Book

Ready-to-Use Templates, Activities, Management Tools, and More — for Every Day of the Month

Karen Sevaly

New York • Toronto • London • Auckland • Sydney
Mexico City • New Delhi • Hong Kong • Buenos Aires

Teaching Resources

DEDICATION
This book is dedicated to teachers and children everywhere.

Cover design by Maria Lilja
Cover art by Jillian Phillips
Interior design by Holly Grundon
Illustrations by Karen Sevaly

ISBN 978-0-545-37942-7

1 2 3 4 5 6 7 8 9 10   40   19 18 17 16 15 14 13

CONTENTS

FAVORITE TOPICS

FLAG DAY

Reproducible Patterns

FATHER'S DAY

FROGS AND CRITTERS WITH SHELLS AND TAILS

CONTENTS

UNDER THE SEA

AWARDS, INCENTIVES, AND MORE

Reproducible Patterns

INTRODUCTION

Welcome to the original Monthly Idea Book series! This book was written especially for teachers getting ready to teach topics related to the month of June.

Each book in this month-by-month series is filled with dozens of ideas for PreK–3 classrooms. Activities connect to the Common Core State Standards for Reading (Foundational Skills), among other subjects, to help you meet the needs of your students. (For more information, see page 16.)

Most everything you need to prepare the lessons and activities in this resource is included, such as:

- calendar and weather-related props

- book cover patterns and stationery for writing assignments

- booklet patterns

- games and puzzles that support learning in curriculum areas such as math, science, and writing

- activity sheets that help students organize information, respond to learning, and explore topics in a meaningful way

- patterns for projects that connect to holidays, special occasions, and commemorative events

All year long, you can weave the ideas and reproducible patterns in these unique books into your monthly lesson plans and classroom activities. Happy teaching!

What's Inside

You'll find that this book is
chockfull of reproducibles
that make lesson planning easier:

■ puppets and
picture props

■ bookmarks, booklets,
and book covers

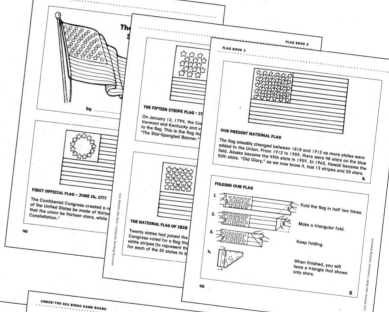

■ game boards and puzzles

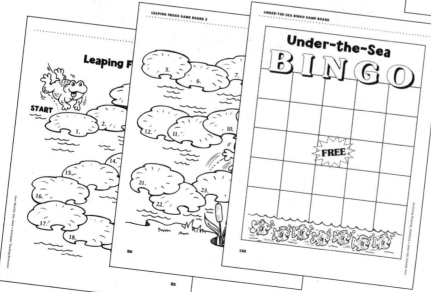

■ stationery and
cards

■ awards and certificates

How to Use This Book

The reproducible pages in this book have flexible use and may be modified to meet your particular classroom needs. Use the reproducible activity pages and patterns in conjunction with the suggested activities provided or weave them into your curriculum in other ways.

★ PHOTOCOPY OR SCAN

To get started, think about your developing lesson plans and upcoming bulletin boards. If desired, carefully remove the pages you will need. Duplicate those pages on copy paper, color paper, tagboard, or overhead transparency sheets. If you have access to a scanner, consider saving the pattern pages as PDF files. That way you can size images up or down and customize them with text to create individualized lessons, center-time activities, interactive whiteboard lessons, homework pages, and more.

LAMINATE FOR DURABILITY

Laminating the reproducibles will help you extend their use. If you have access to a roll laminator, then you already know how fortunate you are when it comes to saving time and resources. If you don't have a laminator, clear adhesive vinyl covering works well. Just sandwich the pattern between two sheets of vinyl and cut off any excess. Then try some of these ideas:

- Put laminated sheets of stationery in a writing center to use for handwriting practice. Wipe-off markers work great on coated pages and can easily be erased with dry tissue.

- Add longevity to calendars, weather-related pictures, and pocket chart rebus pictures by preserving them with lamination.

- Transform picture props into flannel board figures. After lamination, add a tab of hook-and-loop fastener to the back of the props and invite students to adhere them to the flannel board for storytelling fun.

- To enliven magnet board activities, affix sections of magnet tape to the back of picture props. Then encourage students to sort images according to the skills you're working on. For example, you might have them group images by commonalities such as initial sound, habitat, or physical attributes.

★ BULLETIN BOARDS

1. Set the Stage

Use background paper colors that complement many themes and seasons. For example, the dark background you use as a spooky display in October will have dramatic effect in November, when you begin a unit on woodland animals or Thanksgiving.

While paper works well, there are other background options available. You might also try fabric from a colorful bed sheet or gingham material. Discontinued rolls of patterned wallpaper can be purchased at discount stores. What's more, newspapers are easy to use and readily available. Attach a background of comics to set off a lesson on riddles, or use grocery store flyers to provide food for thought on a bulletin board about nutrition.

2. Make the Display

The reproducible patterns in this book can be enlarged to fit your needs. When we say enlarge, we mean it! Think BIG! Use an overhead projector to enlarge the images you need to make your bulletin board extraordinary.

If your school has a stencil press, you're lucky. The rest of us can use these strategies for making headers and titles.

- Cut strips of paper, cloud shapes, or cartoon bubbles. They will all look great! Then, by hand, write the text using wide-tipped permanent markers or tempera paint.

- If you must cut individual letters, use 4- by 6-inch pieces of construction paper. (Laminate first, if you can.) Cut the uppercase letters as shown on page 14. No need to measure, as somewhat irregular letters will look creative, not messy.

3. Add Color and Embellishments

Use your imagination! You'll be surprised at the great displays you can create.

- Watercolor markers work great on small areas. On larger areas, you can switch to crayons, color chalk, or pastels. (Lamination will keep the color off of you. No laminator? A little hairspray will do the trick as a fixative.)

- Cut character eyes and teeth from white paper and glue them in place. The features will really stand out and make your bulletin boards engaging.

- For special effects, include items that provide texture and visual interest, such as buttons, yarn, and lace. Try cellophane or blue glitter glue on water scenes. Consider using metallic wrapping paper or aluminum foil to add a bit of shimmer to stars and belt buckles.

- Finally, take a picture of your completed bulletin board. Store the photos in a recipe box or large sturdy envelope. Next year when you want to create the same display, you'll know right where everything goes. You might even want to supply students with pushpins and invite them to recreate the display, following your directions and using the photograph as support.

Staying Organized

Organizing materials with monthly file folders provides you with a location to save reproducible activity pages and patterns, along with related craft ideas, recipes, and magazine or periodical articles.

If you prefer, use file boxes instead of folders. You'll find that with boxes there will plenty of room to store enlarged patterns, sample art projects, bulletin board materials, and much more.

Meeting the Standards

CONNECTIONS TO THE COMMON CORE STATE STANDARDS

The Common Core State Standards Initiative (CCSSI) has outlined learning expectations in English/Language Arts, among other subject areas, for students at different grade levels. In general, the activities in this book align with the following standards for students in grades K–3. For more information, visit the CCSSI website at www.corestandards.org.

Reading: Foundational Skills

Print Concepts
- RF.K.1, RF.1.1. Demonstrate understanding of the organization and basic features of print.

Phonics and Word Recognition
- RF.K.3, RF.1.3, RF.2.3, RF.3.3. Know and apply grade-level phonics and word analysis skills in decoding words.

Fluency
- RF.K.4. Read emergent-reader texts with purpose and understanding.
- RF.1.4, RF.2.4, RF.3.4. Read with sufficient accuracy and fluency to support comprehension.

Writing

Production and Distribution of Writing
- W.3.4. Produce writing in which the development and organization are appropriate to task and purpose.
- W.K.5, W.1.5, W.2.5, W.3.5. Focus on a topic and strengthen writing as needed by revising and editing.

Research to Build and Present Knowledge
- W.K.7, W.1.7, W.2.7. Participate in shared research and writing projects.
- W.3.7. Conduct short research projects that build knowledge about a topic.
- W.K.8, W.1.8, W.2.8, W.3.8. Recall information from experiences or gather information from provided sources to answer a question.

Range of Writing
- W.3.10. Write routinely over extended time frames (time for research, reflection, and revision) and shorter time frames (a single sitting or a day or two) for a range of discipline-specific tasks, purposes, and audiences.

Speaking & Listening

Comprehension and Collaboration
- SL.K.1, SL.1.1, SL.2.1. Participate in collaborative conversations with diverse partners about grade-level topics and texts with peers and adults in small and larger groups.
- SL.K.2, SL.1.2, SL.2.2, SL.3.2. Recount or describe key ideas or details from a text read aloud or information presented orally or through other media.
- SL.K.3, SL.1.3, SL.2.3, SL.3.3. Ask and answer questions about what a speaker says in order to gather additional information or clarify something that is not understood.

Presentation of Knowledge and Ideas
- SL.K.4, SL.1.4, SL.2.4. Describe people, places, things, and events with relevant details, expressing ideas and feelings clearly.
- SL.K.5, SL.1.5, SL.2.5, SL.3.5. Add drawings or other visual displays to stories or recounts of experiences when appropriate to clarify ideas, thoughts, and feelings.

Language

Conventions of Standard English
- L.K.1, L.1.1, L.2.1, L.3.1. Demonstrate command of the conventions of standard English grammar and usage when writing or speaking.
- L.K.2, L.1.2, L.2.2, L.3.2. Demonstrate command of the conventions of standard English capitalization, punctuation, and spelling when writing.

Knowledge of Language
- L.2.3, L.3.3. Use knowledge of language and its conventions when writing, speaking, reading, or listening.

Vocabulary Acquisition and Use
- L.K.4, L.1.4, L.2.4, L.3.4. Determine or clarify the meaning of unknown and multiple-meaning words and phrases based on grade level reading and content, choosing flexibly from an array of strategies.
- L.K.6, L.1.6, L.2.6, L.3.6. Use words and phrases acquired through conversations, reading and being read to, and responding to texts.

CALENDAR TIME

Getting Started

June Monthly Idea Book • Scholastic Teaching Resources

June

Sunday	Monday	Tuesday	Wednesday	Thursday	Friday	Saturday

19

CALENDAR

★ MARK YOUR CALENDAR

Make photocopies of the calendar grid on page 19 and use it to meet your needs. Consider using the write-on spaces to:

- write the corresponding numerals for each day

- mark and count how many days have passed

- track the weather with stamps or stickers

- note student birthdays

- record homework assignments

- communicate with families about positive behaviors

- remind volunteers about schedules, field trips, shortened days, and so on

CELEBRATIONS THIS MONTH

Whether you post a photocopy of pages 20 through 23 near your class calendar or just turn to these pages for inspiration, you're sure to find lots of information on them to discuss with students. To take celebrating and learning a step further, invite the class to add more to the list. For example, students can add anniversaries of significant events and the birthdays of their favorite authors or historical figures.

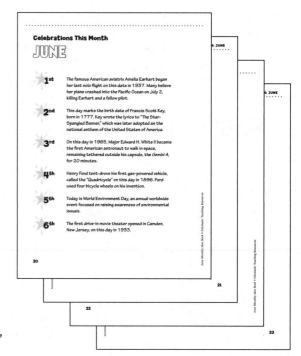

CALENDAR HEADER

You can make a photocopy of the header on page 24, color it, and use it as a title for your classroom calendar. You might opt to give the coloring job to a student who has a birthday that month. The student is sure to enjoy seeing his or her artwork each and every day of the month.

BEFORE INTRODUCING WHAT'S THE WEATHER?

Make a photocopy of the body template on page 25. Laminate it so you can use it again and again. Before sharing the template with the class, cut out pieces of cloth in the shapes of clothing students typically wear this month. For example, if you live in a warm weather climate, your June attire might include shorts and t-shirts. If you live in chillier climates, your attire might include a scarf, hat, and coat. Fit the cutouts to the body outline. When the clothing props are made, and you're ready to have students dress the template, display the clothing. Invite the "weather helper of the day" to tell what pieces of clothing he or she would choose to dress appropriately for the weather. (For extra fun, use foam to cut out accessories such as an umbrella, sunhat, and raincoat.)

June

Sunday	Monday	Tuesday	Wednesday	Thursday	Friday	Saturday

Celebrations This Month

JUNE

1st The famous American aviatrix Amelia Earhart began her last solo flight on this date in 1937. Many believe her plane crashed into the Pacific Ocean on July 2, killing Earhart and a fellow pilot.

2nd This day marks the birth date of Francis Scott Key, born in 1777. Key wrote the lyrics to "The Star-Spangled Banner," which was later adopted as the national anthem of the United States of America.

3rd On this day in 1965, Major Edward H. White II became the first American astronaut to walk in space, remaining tethered outside his capsule, the *Gemini 4*, for 20 minutes.

4th Henry Ford test-drove his first gas-powered vehicle, called the "Quadricycle" on this day in 1896. Ford used four bicycle wheels on his invention.

5th Today is World Environment Day, an annual worldwide event focused on raising awareness of environmental issues.

6th The first drive-in movie theater opened in Camden, New Jersey, on this day in 1933.

June Monthly Idea Book © Scholastic Teaching Resources

7th   On this day in 1889, Hudson Stuck led the first expedition to reach the peak of Alaska's Mount McKinley, the highest point in North America.

8th   Frank Lloyd Wright, American architect and interior designer, was born on this day in 1867.

9th   American composer and songwriter Cole Porter was born on this day in 1891. Porter wrote lyrics and music for many Broadway musicals.

10th   Maurice Sendak, author of the beloved children's book *Where the Wild Things Are*, was born on this day in 1928.

11th   Famous oceanographer and author Jacques Cousteau was born on this day in 1910.

12th   Today marks the birth date of Anne Frank, born in 1929. Frank's father published *Diary of a Young Girl*, a personal account of Anne's life in hiding during the German occupation of the Netherlands in World War II.

13th   On this day in 1967, President Johnson appointed Thurgood Marshall to the Supreme Court, making him the first African-American Supreme Court Justice.

14th   Today is Flag Day, a national day of observance held annually to commemorate the adoption by Congress of the first flag of the United States.

15th On this day in 1836, Arkansas became the 25th state of the United States of America.

16th America's first roller coaster opened on this day in 1884. The "thrill" ride, located at Coney Island, cost a nickel to ride.

17th The Statue of Liberty, a gift to America from the people of France, arrived by ship in New York Harbor on this day in 1885.

18th Sally Ride became the first American woman to travel into space on this day in 1983.

19th The comic strip "Garfield," created by Jim Davis, debuted on this day in 1978.

20th Samuel Morse was granted a patent for the telegraph on this day in 1840.

21st On this day in 1788, the Constitution of the United States was ratified, making it the law of the land.

22nd On this day in 1970, President Nixon signed a bill to lower the voting age for all federal, state, and local elections in the United States from 21 years of age to 18.

23rd Wilma Rudolph, three-time Olympic gold medalist at the 1960 Olympic Games, was born on this day in 1940.

24th On this day in 1916, film star Mary Pickford became the first female to sign a million dollar contract.

June Monthly Idea Book © Scholastic Teaching Resources

25th Columbia Broadcasting System (CBS) aired the first color television show on this day in 1951.

26th On this day in 1974, the first Universal Product Code (UPC) was scanned at a supermarket in Ohio. The code was on a package of chewing gum.

27th Helen Keller, American author, lecturer, and first deaf-blind person to earn a Bachelor of Arts degree, was born on this day in 1880. Keller's life was featured in the film *The Miracle Worker*.

28th The Treaty of Versailles, which ended World War I exactly five years after it began, was signed on this day in 1919.

29th On this day in 1995, the largest man-made satellite to orbit the earth was formed when the space shuttle *Atlantis* docked with the Russian space station *Mir*.

30th The United States Fish and Wildlife Service was established on this day in 1940.

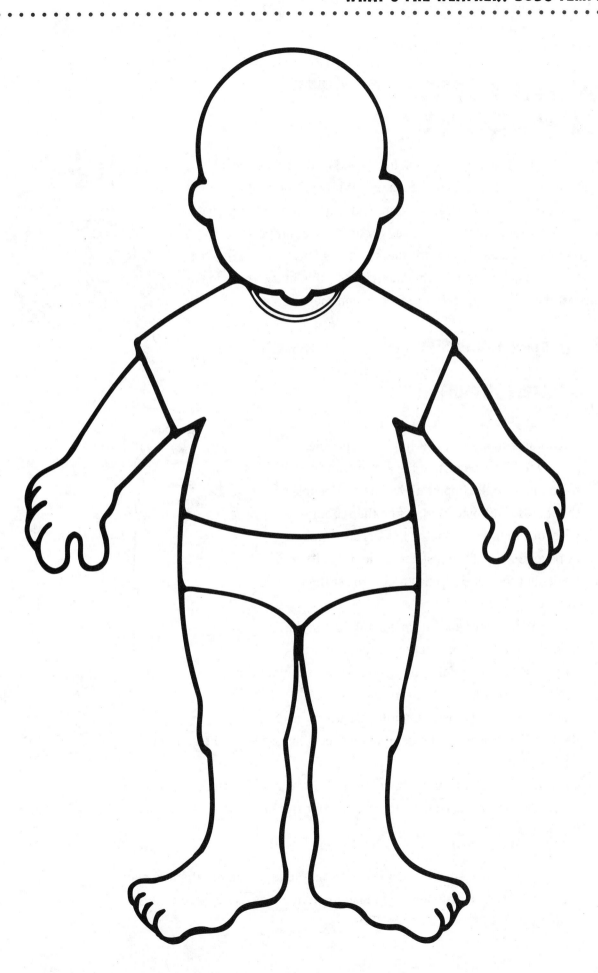

WRAPPING UP THE SCHOOL YEAR

Teachers and students alike look to the end of the school year with great anticipation and excitement. While celebrations are in order for a year full of class learning and achievement, the final weeks are also an ideal time to review and reflect on personal accomplishments and goals for the future. As you wrap up the year with students, use the ideas and activities in this unit to help make the last days of school both productive and memorable.

Suggested Activities

 ## MY MEMORY BOOK

A school year is often filled with fun times, memorable moments, and important people. Invite students to create a book of memories to summarize the important events and people that helped influence and define the school year for them. First, photocopy a class supply of pages 30–34. Then distribute the pages to students (one set per child) and instruct them to follow these directions:

cover: Write your grade on the blank line in the title. Fill in the bottom section of the cover.

page 1: Fill in the information about your school and the people who work or volunteer there.

page 2: Write about your favorite things on this page.

page 3: Invite several friends to write special messages and sign their names on the notes.

page 4: Fill in information about yourself. Draw a self-portrait or glue your school picture in the picture frame. Ask your teacher to write a message in the bottom section and sign it.

To complete, have students staple their pages together. Invite them to share their books with classmates, then take them home as a keepsake of their school year.

END-OF-YEAR WRITING

Invite students to complete the following creative writing assignments as they reflect on their school year and look forward to their summer vacation.

Welcome to My Grade

Distribute photocopies of page 35 to students and explain that they will use this page to write letters to students who will be assigned next year to the same grade, teacher, and classroom that they now occupy. After completing the page, encourage students to write additional information on the back. For example, they might tell about classroom events, field trips, special classes, interesting people at school, and so on. Fold and place each student's page in an envelope. Then, before the first day of the next school year, write the name of each new student on one of the envelopes and place it in that child's assigned desk or cubby. Your new students will be delighted to be greeted with a letter that foreshadows the wonderful things that await them.

End-of-Year Letter to My Teacher

Invite students to write a letter to you on photocopies of the stationery on page 36. They might include special memories about you, the class, or school. Or, they might write suggestions about things you might keep the same, change, or improve in your class to help make the upcoming school year more enjoyable for your new students.

My Summer Wish

Students can use photocopies of page 37 to write about their hopes, wishes, and plans for the summer vacation. You might place a supply of this stationery in your writing center so students can use more than one sheet, if needed, to complete their writing.

SUMMER POSTCARDS

Explain that students will design postcards that you will send to them after school ends. First, have them illustrate one side of a plain 4- by 6-inch index card with crayons or colored pencils. They might draw a picture of the school, a favorite class activity, or something they anticipate seeing or doing on their vacation. Then have students self-address a mailing label and attach it to the right side of the back of their cards. Collect the postcards and set them aside. After the last day, write a personal message on each student's postcard and drop it into the mail. Students will be thrilled to get a special note in the mail from their teacher!

BROWN BAG PACK-UP

Distribute large, brown paper grocery bags to students. Invite them to decorate their bags with crayons, markers, magazine cutouts, and so on. They might also ask classmates to autograph their bags. Then collect the bags and set them aside until the last day of school. On that day, have students use their bag to pack up their personal items, schoolwork, and year-end materials to take home for the summer.

A NOTE TO PARENTS

Send home photocopies of the note on page 38 to offer parents suggestions about how to reinforce and extend their child's learning over the summer months. You might include this note with students' final progress reports or place in a folder or envelope with other important end-of-year information for parents.

GRADUATION PREPARATION

You can use the following activities for a class graduation ceremony or promotion celebration for your students.

Graduate Mortarboards

To make a mortarboard for each child, you'll need the following: 6- by 22-inch sheet of black construction paper, 10-inch square of black poster board, black button, and yarn in the color of your choice (or a school color). Follow these directions to make each mortarboard:

1. Make a tassel from the yarn.

2. Glue the unfringed end of the tassel to the center of the 10-inch poster-board square. Then glue the button on top of that end of the tassel, as shown.

3. For the headband, fit the 6- by 22-inch construction paper around the child's head, staple the ends in place, and trim as needed.

4. Cut a "widow's peak" shape along one edge long edge of the headband, as shown. This will be the front of the mortarboard.

5. Cut slits about 1-inch long along the other long edge of the headband. Space the slits evenly, leaving about 1 1/4 inches between them, as shown.

6. Fold the slits back and glue to the square, centering the square on the headband.

Invite students to wear their mortarboards during your graduation or promotion ceremony.

Promotion Nametags

Photocopy a class supply of the nametags on page 39. Then invite students to color and cut out a nametag, write their name on it, and attach it to their clothing with rolled tape. Or, you might have students add a yarn hanger to their nametag to wear as a necklace.

Promotion Certificate

Fill out a photocopy of the certificate on page 40 for each student. Present the certificates to students at your end-of-year ceremony, adding a personal message as you hand each student the page.

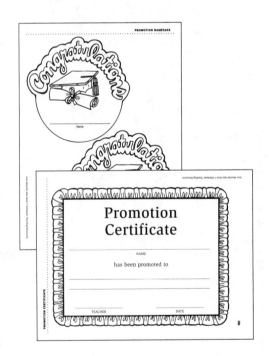

★ CERTIFICATE OF APPRECIATION

Be sure to acknowledge school staff members, parents, and volunteers for their help and contributions to your class throughout the year! To do this, simply fill in a photocopy of page 41 for each person you want to acknowledge, then have students color the art on the certificates. As a class, present the completed certificates to the recipients personally or during an appreciation event held in their honor.

My

Grade

Memory
Book

_____
Student's Name

_____
Teacher

_____   _____
Year   School

Special People at My School

School: _____

_____

Address: _____

_____

My Teacher: _____

Principal: _____

Secretary: _____

School Nurse: _____

Custodian: _____

Bus Driver: _____

Other helpers at my school: _____

_____

_____

_____

_____

1

My _____ Grade Favorites

Subject: _____

Book: _____

Lunch: _____

_____

Recess activity: _____

_____

Special event: _____

_____

Friends: _____

_____

_____

Thing that happened at school this year: _____

_____

_____

_____

_____

2

Comments From My Friends

Signed

Signed

Signed

Signed

Signed

Signed

3

In _____ grade,

I was _____ years old.

I was _____ inches tall.

I wore size _____ shoes.

I had freckles: ☐ yes ☐ no

I wore glasses: ☐ yes ☐ no

I wore braces: ☐ yes ☐ no

My favorite thing to wear

to school was _____

_____

**My School
Picture**

Comments From My Teacher

_____

_____

_____

_____

_____

4

Welcome to Grade _____

You are going to have a great year!

My favorite time in class was

_____

_____

To have a successful year, you will need to:

1. _____

2. _____

3. _____

My favorite book was _____

_____

The most important rule to follow is _____

_____

My favorite thing to do at recess was _____

_____

Make sure you always _____

_____

Have a great year!

_____
Signature

An End-of-Year Letter to My Teacher

_____
Date

Dear _____,

_____

_____

_____

_____

_____

_____

_____

_____

_____

_____

                                    _____
                                    Signed

June Monthly Idea Book © Scholastic Teaching Resources

My Wish for a
Great Summer!

Ways You Can Help Your Child This Summer!

As a parent, there are many things you can do this summer to help your child retain what he or she has learned during this school year. Here are a few ideas:

• Make regular visits to the public library and encourage your child to read daily.

• Visit local museums and cultural centers. Take time to discuss with your child what he or she learned from the visit.

• Help your child get regular physical exercise. Consider signing your child up for activities such as swimming lessons, karate classes, dance sessions, or a team sport.

• Limit your child's television viewing to a specific amount of time per day. Help your child choose age-appropriate programs to watch.

• Try to incorporate math, reading, and spelling practice in your child's daily activities. You might purchase or make flash cards. Keep the learning fun and enjoyable for your child.

• Encourage your child to take up a hobby, such as collecting rocks, insects, or seashells. Help him or her find and read information about the hobby.

• Play board games, act out plays, sing songs, and make simple recipes with your child. As you do these fun activities, emphasize reading and math skills as opportunities arise.

• Give your child a new notebook or blank book to use for a daily journal. Encourage him or her to write in the journal every day.

• Read to, or with, your child daily.

• Spend some quiet time each day talking to your child about things that are important to him or her. Praise your child for his or her efforts, uniqueness, and special qualities.

Have a safe and happy summer!

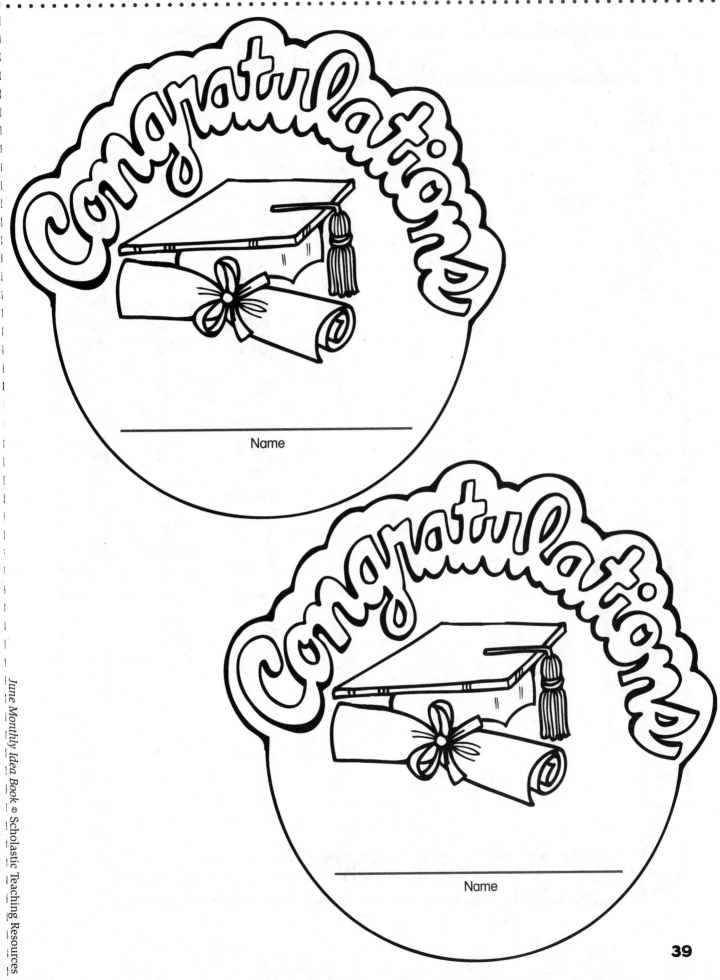

Name

Name

Promotion Certificate

NAME

has been promoted to

TEACHER

DATE

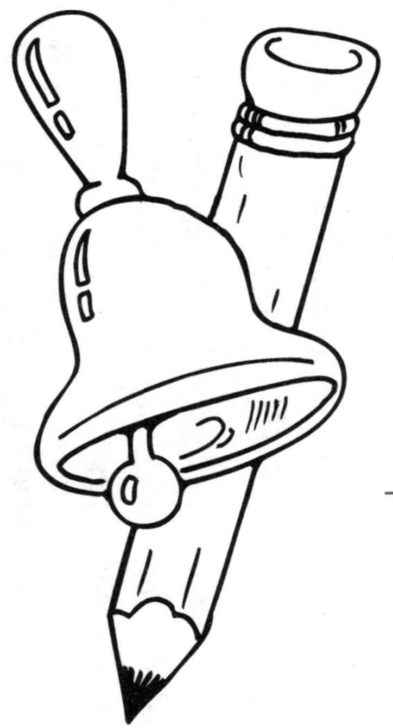

Certificate of Appreciation

given to

_____
Name

in appreciation for your
valuable contribution of

_____

_____
Date

_____'s class

_____
Teacher

FLAG DAY

In 1916, Bernard Cigrand, the son of Luxembourg immigrants, saw a lifelong dream come true: President Wilson issued a proclamation calling for a nationwide observance of Flag Day to be held on June 14. More than 30 years after Wilson's proclamation, President Truman signed an Act of Congress designating the 14th of June every year as National Flag Day.

The movement to honor our flag began in 1885 when Cigrand held the first formal observance of Flag Day in his hometown of Waubeka, Wisconsin. From that point forward, Cigrand devoted his time and energy to advocating for a national holiday to honor and show respect for the flag. He wrote letters, authored hundreds of magazine and newspaper articles, and made numerous speeches. Due to the tireless efforts of Cigrand, often called "The Father of Flag Day," June 14 is now a day on which the American flag flies proudly on public and private buildings throughout the nation as citizens celebrate the symbolism, history, and country that it represents.

Flag Facts

- The Continental Congress passed the first Flag Act on June 14, 1777, stating: "Resolved, That the flag of the United States be made of thirteen stripes, alternate red and white; that the union be thirteen stars, white in a blue field, representing a new Constellation."

- The flag is also called the Stars and Stripes.

- The red, white, and blue colors of the flag were not assigned any specific meanings when it was adopted in 1777.

- The flag has featured 13 stripes throughout most of its history. However, the arrangement and number of stars on the flag has changed over time.

- While the red and white stripes on our current flag continue to represent the thirteen original colonies (one stripe per colony), the number of stars has increased to fifty (one for each of the fifty states).

- All official U.S. flags meet standard size proportions.

- The field of stars on the blue background is called the *union*.

- The height, or *hoist*, is almost one half the length, or *fly*, of the flag.

June Monthly Idea Book © Scholastic Teaching Resources

Suggested Activities

 ### FLAG MINI-BOOK

Explain to students that the design of the U.S. flag changed over time as our nation grew and admitted new states. However, the flag colors have always been red, white, and blue. After sharing about the evolution of the first flag to its current design, invite students to create a mini-book featuring some of the history and changes of the American flag. First, photocopy a class supply of the mini-book patterns on pages 46–48. Distribute a set of pages to each student. Then have students color and cut apart their pages. Remind them that the stripes should be colored in an alternating red and white pattern and the field behind the stars should be blue. Finally, have students sequence and staple their pages together along the left edge.

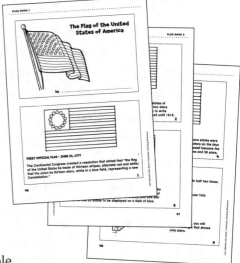

After students complete their mini-books, review the last page with them. If possible, provide a flag and invite student pairs or small groups take turns folding the flag following the directions on page 5 of the mini-book.

 ### THE PLEDGE OF ALLEGIANCE

Ask students if they know The Pledge of Allegiance to the Flag. Explain that this 31-word pledge is an expression of loyalty to the flag and the United States of America. Then write the pledge on the chalkboard or chart paper. As you read the pledge aloud, circle words that students may not be familiar with or that you want to point out as part of a word-study unit. For example, you might circle *pledge, allegiance, republic, indivisible, liberty,* and *justice.* After reviewing the entire text, revisit the circled words and discuss their meanings. If desired, add these words to a word wall along with other Flag-Day-related words that students might hear or use (such as *patriotism, hoist,* and *salute*). Then refer students to the word wall to find words to use in writing assignments about the flag.

The Pledge of Allegiance to the Flag

I pledge allegiance to the flag of the United States of America, and to the republic for which it stands, one nation under God, indivisible, with liberty and justice for all.

★ COLORS OF THE FLAG

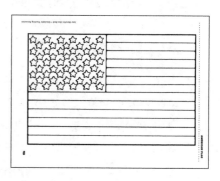

Distribute photocopies of the flag on page 49. Explain that this flag represents the current official flag of the United States with its thirteen stripes and fifty stars. Then ask students to color the flag, using the official colors of red, white, and blue. If desired, make available a variety of coloring tools and craft items for students to use when decorating their flags. For instance, you might provide glitter crayons or pens, puff-paint pens, glitter, sequins, small buttons, pompoms, yarn, and torn tissue paper.

Encourage students to use the items of their choice to fill in the appropriate colors in the proper areas of their flag. Afterward, invite students to display their flags on a class bulletin board titled "Hooray for the Red, White, and Blue!"

★ FLAG ETIQUETTE

Tell students that the flag code contains specific ways to display, show respect for, and dispose of the national flag. Share a few of these rules, known as flag etiquette (see below). If desired, visit a website such as www.usflag.org/flagetiquette.html to learn more about the American flag.

■ When lowering the flag, no part of it should touch the ground.

■ Nothing should ever be placed on or above the flag.

■ When displaying the American flag with a group of other flags, it should be at the center of the group and flown higher than the other flags.

■ To salute the flag, nonmilitary citizens should stand and place their right hand over their heart. Men should remove their hat and hold it with their right hand over their heart.

★ FLAG DAY STATIONERY

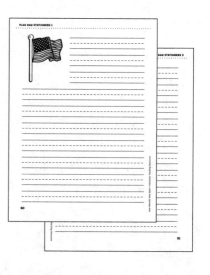

Liven up students' writing with stationery ideal for writing about Flag Day, the American flag, the history of our flag, showing respect for the flag, what the flag means to them, how they celebrate Flag Day, or other related topics. Students might write poems, songs, acrostics, or imaginary stories. Distribute copies of the stationery on page 50 for students to use for their final drafts. Then invite volunteers to share their written work with small groups or the whole class.

In addition, students can use the stationery on page 51 to write about why they are proud to live in America, ways to show patriotism, how they participate in patriotic holidays, and so on.

FLAG DAY FUN GLASSES

Invite students to make and wear a pair of glasses to celebrate Flag Day. Distribute copies of the glasses patterns on page 52. Ask students to color the patterns in the colors of the flag: red, white, and blue. Then have them cut out the pieces, carefully cutting out the centers of the glasses (for lenses) and the slits on the glasses frame and the earpieces. To assemble, students simply fit each earpiece into the corresponding slit on the frame. If desired, students can take their glasses home to share with family members.

PATRIOTIC HAT

As part of their Flag Day festivities, students can make patriotic hats that sport stars and stripes as found on the American flag. First, distribute copies of the hat pattern on page 53. Ask students to color the stripes in a red and white alternating pattern. Then have them color the hatband blue. They can also color the hat brim blue, or red, if preferred. (Students should leave the stars white.) Next, have students cut out their hat and staple the cutout to a 2- by 24-inch strip of blue construction paper. To complete, help students fit the strip to their head, stapling the ends together and trimming the excess. Invite students to wear their patriotic hat during your class Flag Day activities.

MINIATURE FLAGS

Invite students to make miniature flags to use in a variety of ways, such as to display on a class bulletin board, border a landscaped area at school on Flag Day, mount on headbands that can be worn in a class parade, display on a refrigerator or message board at home, or just to wave on Flag Day. To make the flags, distribute copies of page 54. Have students cut out each flag, color it (red, white, and blue), and attach a craft-stick flagpole.

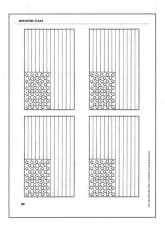

The Flag of the United States of America

by _____

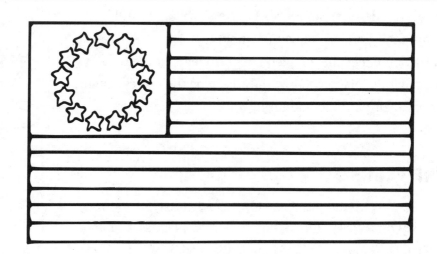

FIRST OFFICIAL FLAG – JUNE 14, 1777

The Continental Congress created a resolution that stated that "the flag of the United States be made of thirteen stripes, alternate red and white; that the union be thirteen stars, white in a blue field, representing a new Constellation."

1

June Monthly Idea Book © Scholastic Teaching Resources

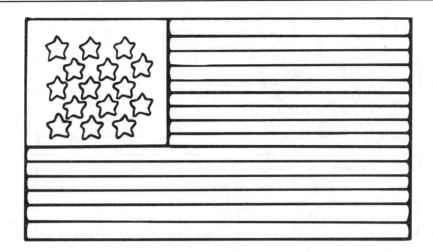

THE FIFTEEN STRIPE FLAG – 1794

On January 13, 1794, the Congress recognized the new states of Vermont and Kentucky and voted to add two stripes and two stars to the flag. This is the flag that inspired Francis Scott Key to write "The Star-Spangled Banner." This flag remained unchanged until 1818.

2

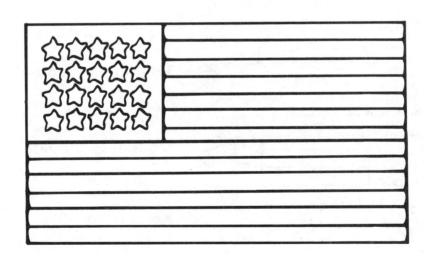

THE NATIONAL FLAG OF 1818

Twenty states had joined the Union by 1818. On April 18th, the Congress voted for a flag that featured 13 alternating red and white stripes (to represent the original 13 states) and one star for each of the 20 states to be displayed on a field of blue.

3

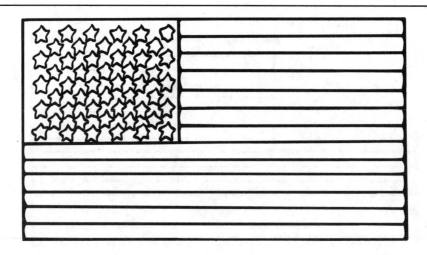

OUR PRESENT NATIONAL FLAG

The flag steadily changed between 1818 and 1912 as more states were added to the Union. From 1912 to 1959, there were 48 stars on the blue field. Alaska became the 49th state in 1959. In 1960, Hawaii became the 50th state. "Old Glory," as we now know it, has 13 stripes and 50 stars.

4

FOLDING OUR FLAG

1. 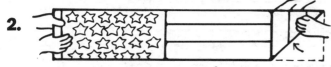 Fold the flag in half two times.

2. 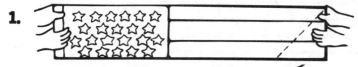 Make a triangular fold.

3.  Keep folding.

4. 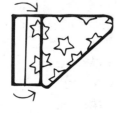 When finished, you will have a triangle that shows only stars.

5

June Monthly Idea Book © Scholastic Teaching Resources

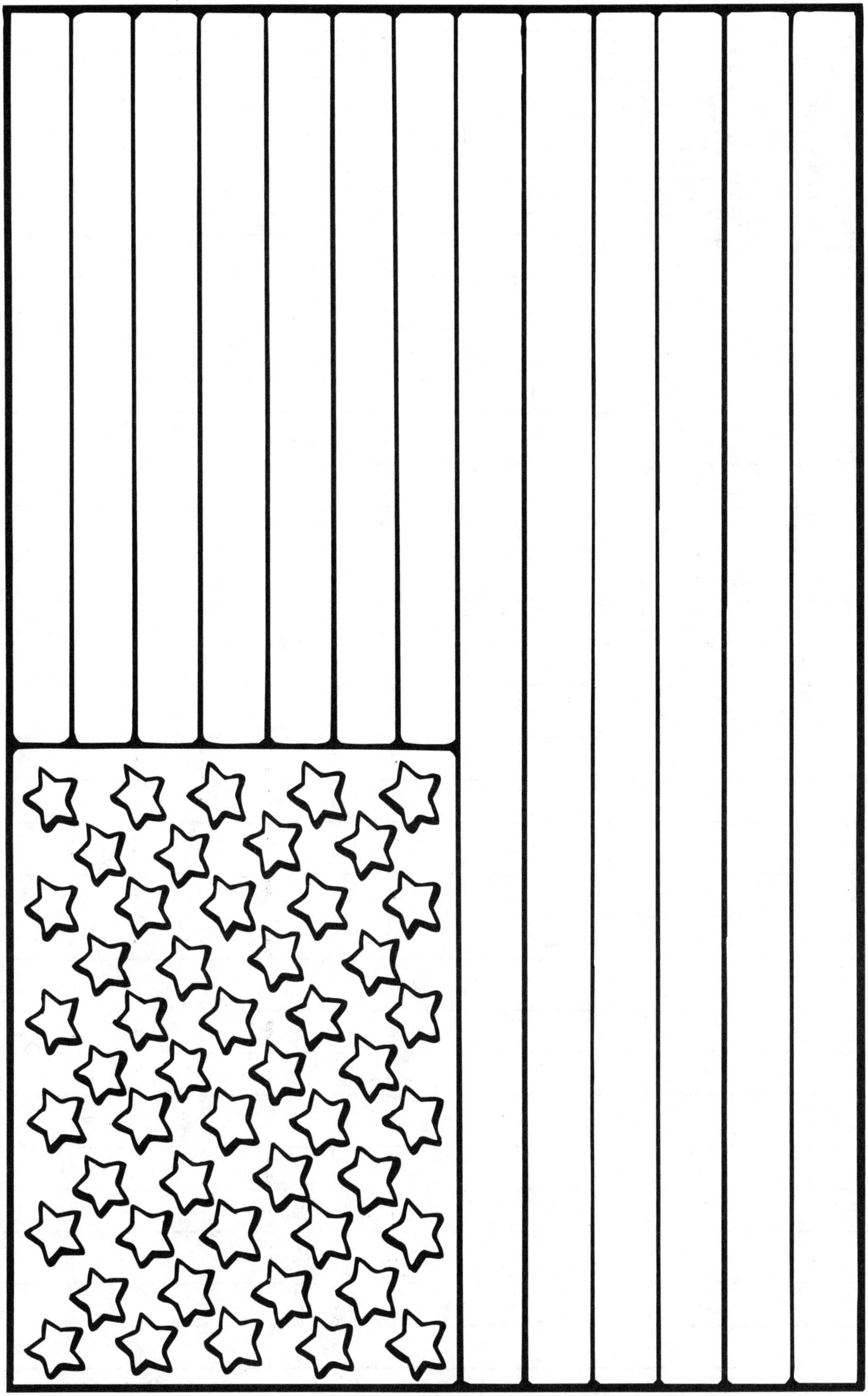

CUT OUT.

CUT OUT.

A

B

B

A

June Monthly Idea Book © Scholastic Teaching Resources

FATHER'S DAY

In 1909, Sonora Louise Smart Dodd of Spokane, Washington, began an effort to devote a special day to honor all fathers, much like Mother's Day. When Dodd was 16 years old, her mother died in childbirth, leaving Dodd to help her father raise her five younger brothers. Dodd watched her father care for his children with great devotion and sacrifice. The high esteem she held for her father led her to present the idea to celebrate a Father's Day to a local ministerial organization and the Young Men's Christian Association (YMCA). With the support of these two groups, Spokane observed the first Father's Day on June 19, 1910, two weeks after her father's birthday.

In a few short years, interest grew across the country for setting aside a time to recognize the important role of fathers. In 1924, President Coolidge supported the idea of observing a national Father's Day, but it wasn't until 1966 that a presidential proclamation was signed by Lyndon B. Johnson to declare national recognition of this day. In 1972, President Nixon established the third Sunday in June as the permanent date to observe Father's Day nationwide. Today, children in the United States honor their fathers with gifts, cards, and many other expressions of affection and gratitude on this special day. While you explore this holiday with students, be sure to communicate reverence and respect for all men who serve as father figures in the home or community.

Suggested Activities

 ## A SPECIAL DAD

Encourage students to reflect on what their father (or father-figure) means to them. *Why is this man special? What do they like most about him? What do they do together that brings each of them joy?* Invite students to share some thoughts about their father with the class. Then distribute photocopies of pages 60 and 61 to students. To begin, have them fill out page 60 by writing some specific things about their dad and the relationship they have with him. Then have students complete the acronym on page 61, using each letter in the word "Father" as the first letter of a word (or phrase) that describes their own father. At the bottom of that page, have students write their definition of a great dad. When finished, encourage volunteers to share their work with the class. Then have students fold their pages, place them in an envelope, and take them home to give to their father.

★ KEYS FOR DAD

Dads can use these keys to unlock special promises. To make, distribute several photocopies of page 62 to each student. (You might copy the pattern onto colored paper.) Have students cut out each key, write a promise to their dad to complete the sentence, and sign their name. Their promises might include performing chores, improving behavior, changing a habit, or doing something special for their dad. When finished, help students cut out the small circle on their keys. Or, have them use a hole punch to remove the circle. Then have students bind the keys together with a metal ring or short length of yarn. Finally, send the keys home with students to give to their dad on Father's Day.

★ FATHER'S DAY POCKET

A pocketful of warm wishes and promises make a great Father's Day surprise. For this project, give each student a photocopy of pages 63 and 64 and a colored sheet of construction paper. Then have students do the following:

1. Cut out all of the patterns.

2. Fold the construction paper in half. Glue the left edge of the pocket cutout along the fold. Trim around the pocket, cutting through all layers.

3. Glue (or staple) together the bottom and right sides of the pocket, leaving the top edge open.

4. Sign the pocket. Write a Father's Day message or pledge on the pencil, pen, and ruler. Put the pieces into the pocket.

FATHER'S DAY COUPON BOOK

Invite students to make this clever coupon book to give on Father's Day. First, distribute photocopies of pages 65–68 to students. Have them color and cut apart the cover and coupons, then complete the sentence on each coupon. Students can write their own text on the blank coupons. (Have students choose the coupons that apply to them and their father and use as many of the blank coupons as desired.) Once done, have students punch holes, where indicated, along the left side of the cover and coupons. Then instruct them to stack their coupons behind the cover and bind them together with ribbon or yarn, as shown.

PERFECT PICTURE FRAME

This simple picture frame makes a wonderful gift for Dad. To make, have students color and cut out tagboard photocopies of the frame pattern on page 69. (If desired, use reduced copies of the pattern for smaller frames.) Then instruct them to carefully cut out the center opening of the frame. Students can bring in a picture of their father or draw a picture to glue to the opening of the frame. Next, have students back the picture with a piece of tagboard that's been cut slightly smaller than the actual frame. For a stand, have students cut out a large triangle from the tagboard piece that was removed from the frame opening. Help them fold back one long edge of the triangle to make a tab, then glue the tab to the back of the frame, as shown.

A DAD BADGE

Invite students to make special badges for their dad and other father figures to wear on their special day. Distribute photocopies of the badges on page 70, giving students as many as they would like to prepare for the men in their life. Have students sign the badges, then color and cut them out. Then help students attach a piece of double-sided tape to each badge, peeling away the backing on only one side to affix it to the badge. Explain that they can remove the outer backing when they are ready to "pin" the badge onto their dad's clothing. If desired, students can tuck their badge into a card as an extra surprise for their dad on his special day.

CARDS FOR DAD!

Children love making cards, and dads love receiving them! Here are some cards kids are sure to enjoy making for the dad in their life.

A Tie for Dad

Provide students with long strips of sturdy, patterned wrapping paper or wallpaper. (You might purchase discontinued or damaged rolls of wallpaper at a reduced price from a hardware or paint store.) Have students cut a V at one end to shape the bottom of their tie, then fanfold it, as shown. Next, show them how to cut out and attach a white construction-paper collar to the top of the tie. To complete, have students write Father's Day messages along the length of the tie.

Dad's Portrait

Have students draw a picture of their dad on the front of a folded sheet of construction paper. Then invite them to use craft items to add features such as yarn hair, pipe-cleaner glasses, a gift-wrap-paper bow or tie, and real buttons on the shirt. If desired, students might draw their dad's face on a small paper plate and add features to make a 3-D picture to glue onto the front of their card. To complete, have students write a Father's Day greeting on the front and a special message inside the card.

Dad in the News

For this unique card, ask students to glue a newspaper page to a sheet of construction paper. They might use a newspaper section to match their dad's interest, such as the sports or business section. Have them trim the newspaper to the size of the construction paper, then use bold lettering to write "Dad, you're in the news..." on the front. On the inside, have students write a news-story-like message to their dad, for instance, "I scored a grand slam with a dad like you!"

Briefcase Card

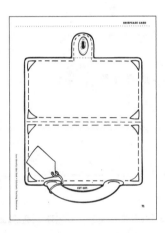

Distribute photocopies of the pattern on page 71 to students. (You might copy the pattern onto sheets of light brown paper.) Then instruct students to cut out the briefcase and carefully cut out the opening under the handle. Next, have them fold their cutout in half along the center line. Students can then write a special message to their dad on the inside of the card and a Father's Day greeting on the outside. If desired, they might also include illustrations. When finished, have students slip the latch through the handle opening and fold it down to "lock" the briefcase.

 ## CERTIFICATE OF ADMIRATION

Many fathers have admirable qualities and do a lot of wonderful things for their family and others. Invite volunteers to share with the class things that they admire about their dad or father figure. Then distribute photocopies of the certificate on page 72 for students to complete for their dad. Send the certificates home with students to present to their dad on Father's Day.

My Dad Is Special!

My dad is special because . . .

_____

_____

_____

_____

I like it when my dad _____

_____

_____

I like to make my dad smile by _____

_____

_____

My dad's favorite thing to do is _____

_____

My dad is smart! He even knows _____

_____

_____

I think my dad is _____

_____

June Monthly Idea Book © Scholastic Teaching Resources

Father's Day Acronym

F _____
_____
A _____
_____
T _____
_____
H _____
_____
E _____
_____
R _____
_____

My definition of a great dad:

_____
_____
_____
_____

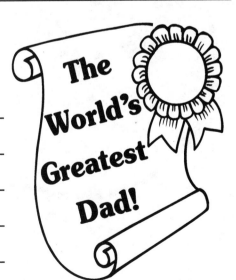

The World's Greatest Dad!

Use this key to unlock my promise to:

Signed

Happy Father's Day!

June Monthly Idea Book © Scholastic Teaching Resources

June Monthly Idea Book © Scholastic Teaching Resources

PLACE THIS SIDE ALONG FOLD.

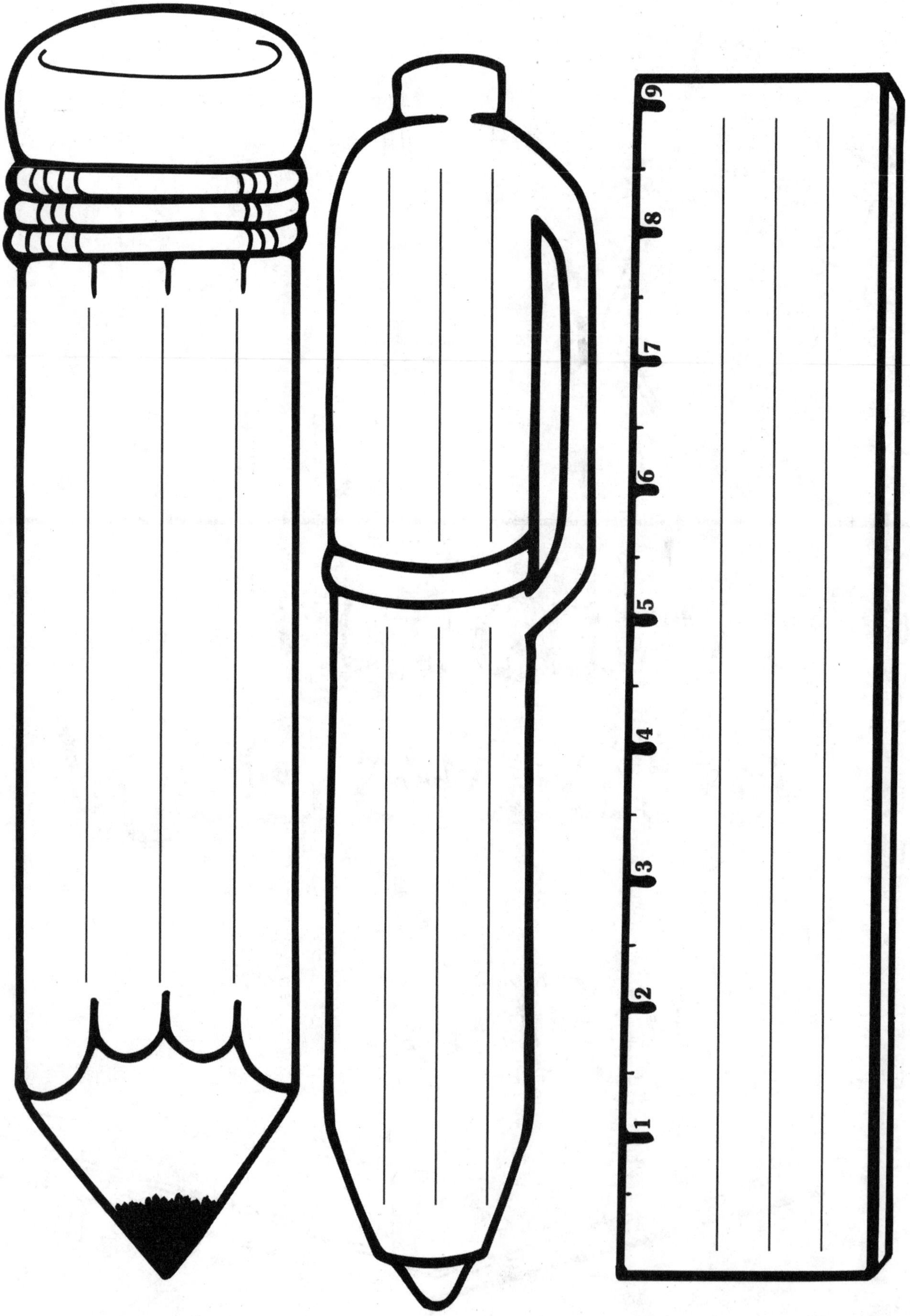

FATHER'S DAY
COUPON BOOK

LOVE, _____

Father's Day Coupon

Redeem this coupon,
and I'll help clean

_____

_____

_____.

Father's Day Coupon

Redeem this coupon, and I'll feed our pets _____ times.

Father's Day Coupon

Redeem this coupon, and I'll help in the kitchen _____ times.

Father's Day Coupon

Redeem this coupon, and I'll help in the garden _____ times.

Father's Day Coupon

Father's Day Coupon

Father's Day Coupon

June Monthly Idea Book © Scholastic Teaching Resources

CUT OUT.

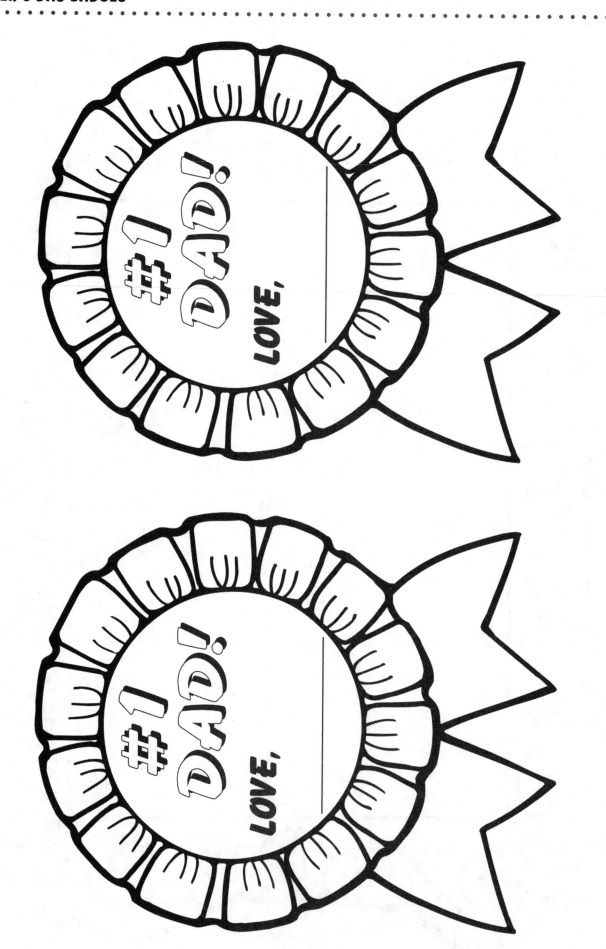

June Monthly Idea Book © Scholastic Teaching Resources

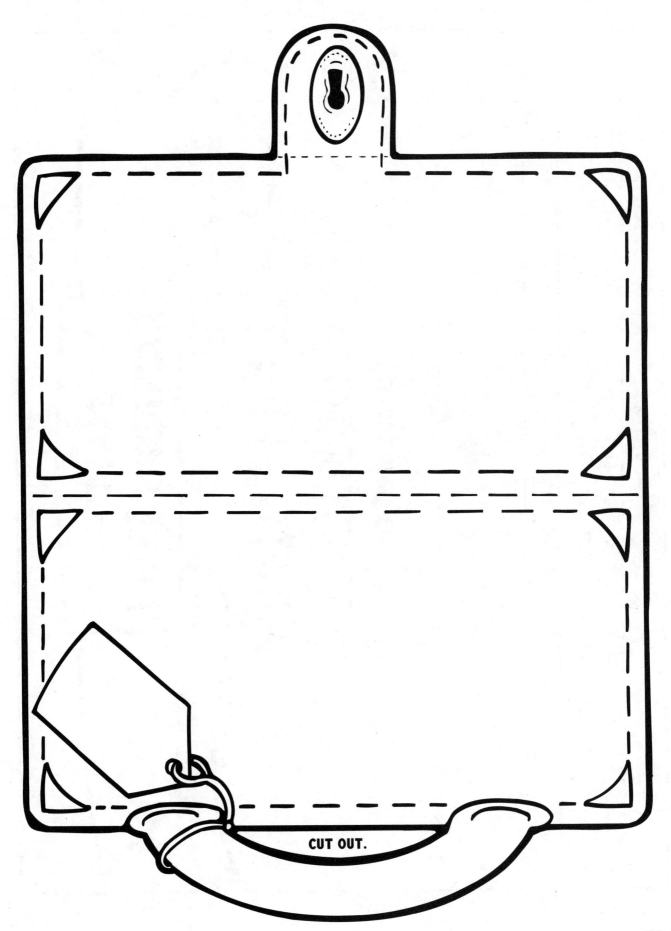

CUT OUT.

HAPPY FATHER'S DAY!

CERTIFICATE
OF ADMIRATION

presented to

for

Love,

Date:

June Monthly Idea Book © Scholastic Teaching Resources

FROGS AND CRITTERS WITH SHELLS AND TAILS

Amphibians and reptiles are common inhabitants of our country's wetland areas. Animals belonging to both groups are cold-blooded—their bodies warm up or cool down with the temperature that surrounds them. Both groups of animals are also vertebrates—they have backbones and bony skeletons. While similar in some ways, there are marked differences between the two animal groups. Frogs and toads, like many amphibians, go through metamorphosis as they develop. On the other hand, reptiles like turtles, snakes, and alligators have babies that look like miniature versions of their parents. As students learn about the amphibians and reptiles in this unit, encourage them to compare and contrast the individual animals and their animal groups.

Suggested Activities

 ### AMPHIBIAN OR REPTILE?

Share with students the characteristics of the amphibian and reptile animal groups. List some animals that belong to each group on chart paper. Then ask students to choose an animal to research. They can use class or library books, the Internet, and other sources to find information about their animal. As students discover facts about their animal, have them complete a photocopy of page 80. When finished, invite them to share their findings with the class.

 ### FASCINATING FROGS!

Tell students that both frogs and toads are amphibians, although they differ in several ways. Then share the frog facts below with students. Afterward, have them do research to learn more about these wonderful wetland creatures. Ask students to use their findings to write a report about frogs, then use the pattern on page 81 to create a book cover for their work. To complete, have students write a title and author line on their cover.

■ A frog has soft, smooth, shiny skin.

■ The diet of a frog consists mainly of insects.

■ A female frog lays eggs in water near vegetation.

- Frog eggs hatch into tadpoles that feed on plants in the water.

- A tadpole lives in water and breathes with gills.

- A tadpole goes through metamorphosis—it changes into a completely different form as it matures.

- As a tadpole grows into a young frog, it develops lungs and begins to spend most of its time on land.

FROG PAPER-BAG PUPPET

Invite students to make frog puppets to use in their presentations. Distribute a small paper bag and a photocopy of the patterns on page 82 to each student. Ask students to color and cut out the patterns. Then have them glue the frog's head to the bottom flap of the bag and the body to the front of the bag below the flap.

THE LIFE CYCLE OF A FROG

Invite students to make a mini-book that describes the metamorphosis of frogs. First, photocopy pages 83 and 84 for each student. Distribute the pages, then review them with students. Invite students to share what they know about frogs and their development as you read each mini-book page and examine the pictures. Afterward, ask students to color, cut apart, and sequence their pages. For a cover, have them fold a half-sheet of construction paper in half, then staple the pages inside the fold along the left edge. Finally, instruct them to add a title and author line to the front cover and embellish both the front and back cover with frog-related art.

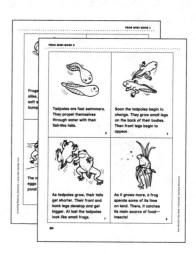

LEAPING FROGS GAME

Use this game for a small-group or learning center activity. Or, make several games and divide the class into groups so they can play at the same time! To get started, photocopy the game boards (pages 85–86). Glue the two parts of the game board together on poster board or to the inside of a file folder. How you use the game and what skills you want students to practice is up to you. Simply write the desired text (or problems) on the spaces of the game board and create task cards to use with the game. Then color the game board and laminate for durability.

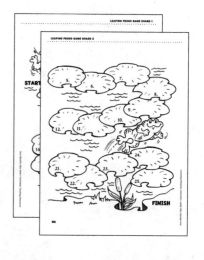

★ FROG AND LILY PAD ACTIVITIES

Photocopy, color, and cut out a supply of the frog and lily pad (page 87) to use for a variety of activities. For example, you might write addition facts on the frogs and sums on the lily pads to create a matching activity. Or, label the cutouts with sight words or vocabulary words for students to use as flash cards. You might also copy the frogs and lily pads onto different colors of paper and have students use them for patterning activities.

★ JUMPING FROG

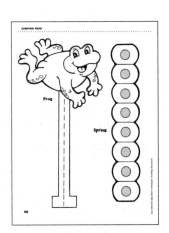

Reinforce graphing concepts with this movement activity. First, divide the class into small groups, each with the same number of students. Explain that each student will take a turn jumping up like a frog. Then have group members keep count as each student jumps in place as many times as possible in a designated amount of time, such as one minute (use a stopwatch or timer). After every student has had a turn to jump, have students add the total number of jumps for their group. Use the results to create a class graph. Then have students use the graph to answer questions, such as "Which group had the most jumps?" and "How many times did groups A and B jump all together?"

As a follow-up, invite students to make a jumping frog. Distribute photocopies of the patterns on page 88, provide scissors and hole punches, then have students do the following to make the project:

1. Cut out the frog and spring patterns.

2. Use a hole punch to remove the circles from the spring. (Younger students may need help punching enough holes to remove each circle entirely.)

3. Fanfold the spring, folding on each of the solid lines.

4. Fold and crease the dashed line on the frog "handle." Insert the handle through the holes in the folded spring.

5. To make the frog "jump," hold the bottom section of the spring between two fingers. Pull the frog handle down through the holes until the frog rests against the folds. Then release the handle—the spring will expand and "shoot" the frog into the air so that it appears to jump!

TURTLE PAPER-BAG PUPPET

Review with students the characteristics of reptiles. (See "Amphibian or Reptile?" on page 73.) Explain that there are four groups of reptiles: turtles and tortoises, snakes and lizards, alligators and crocodiles, and the tuatara, a lizard-like creature in New Zealand that is the only survivor of a group of reptiles that lived during the time of dinosaurs. After sharing, ask students to do research to learn about turtles and tortoises. *What makes these animals distinct from the other groups of reptiles? What are their main characteristics? Where do they live? What do they eat? How do they develop?* Encourage students to write about their findings. (You might form two groups and have one research turtles and the other tortoises.)

Once students complete their written reports, invite them to create turtle puppets to use when presenting their information. To make their puppets, students simply color and cut out photocopies of the patterns on page 89. Then they glue the turtle's head to the bottom flap of a small paper bag and its body to the front of the bag below the flap.

 TURTLE MINI-BOOK

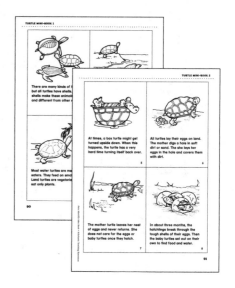

Students can share this fact-filled mini-book about turtles with friends and family. Distribute photocopies of pages 90 and 91 to students. Read aloud the text on the mini-book pages to students, inviting them to share what they know about turtles (and tortoises) as you review and examine the pictures. Afterward, ask students to color, cut apart, and sequence their pages. For a cover, have them fold a half-sheet of construction paper in half, then staple the pages inside the fold along the left edge. Finally, instruct them to add a title and author line to the front cover and embellish both the front and back cover with turtle-related art.

TURTLE PULL-THROUGH

Invite students to make this turtle project to practice a variety of skills. To begin, distribute photocopies of the patterns on page 92. Then instruct them to do the following:

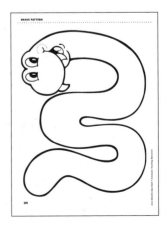

1. Cut out the patterns. Cut slits along the dashed lines at the bottom of the turtle shell.

2. Write a set of skills on the sections of the turtle shell, such as math facts that have the same answer, or words that have the same vowel sound. Leave the section with the slits blank.

3. Thread the turtle's neck through the slits, as shown on page 92. (The right end of this piece will serve as the turtle's tail.)

4. With the head extended on the left side of the shell, write the answer to the skills on the neck that shows between the slits. For example, if the answer to all of the math facts is "6," write that number on the neck.

5. Pull the neck to the right through the slits to hide the head behind the shell.

6. To use, invite classmates to find the common answer to all of the items on the shell, then pull the turtles' head out of the shell to check their answer.

TURTLE SKILLS

Use the turtle pattern on page 93 to encourage students to share their turtle knowledge or reinforce a variety of skills. To make a stick puppet, students can color and cut out photocopies of the pattern and add a craft-stick handle. They can then use the puppet to share turtle facts or as a prop in turtle-related dramatizations. Or, you might label the sections of the turtle shell with math problems (or other skills of your choice, such as sight words or word families), photocopy a class supply of the page, then have students complete the page.

ALL ABOUT SNAKES

Unlike other reptiles, snakes have no legs. How do snakes travel without legs? After students share their ideas, ask small groups to do research to learn how snakes move, as well as what they eat, how they develop, and other facts about these belly-crawlers. Have students cut out photocopies of the snake on page 94 and write their findings on the cutout. Each student might write one or two facts on his or her snake. When finished, invite groups to share their findings.

★ SNAKE STICK PUPPET

Students can use these puppets as props when sharing their snake knowledge at school or home. To make, have students color and cut out photocopies of the snake patterns on page 95. Instruct them to glue the head to one end of a 24-inch length of crepe streamer and the rattle to the other end. Then help them glue a red yarn (or ribbon) tongue to the snake's mouth. To complete, have them attach a craft-stick handle to the head.

★ SNAKY SKILLS GAME

Use this game board to reinforce students' snake knowledge or other skills students need to practice, such as math facts or sight words. First, photocopy the game board on page 96. (If desired, enlarge the game board.) Then write the desired text (or problems) on the spaces of the game board and create task cards to use with the game. Finally, color the game board and laminate for durability. The game can be used as a small-group or learning center activity.

★ STAND-UP ALLIGATOR

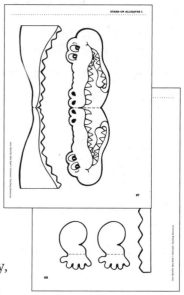

Alligators often catch the interest and imagination of children. Ask students to research these large, scaly reptiles and write a report about their findings. Afterward, invite students to make stand-up alligators to use as props when presenting their reports. First, have them color and cut out tagboard photocopies of the alligator patterns on pages 97–98. Then provide 9-inch squares of tagboard and have students do the following:

1. Fold the tagboard square in half. This will be the alligator's body, with the fold being the top of the body.

2. Glue the zigzag spine to the top of the alligator's body along the fold.

3. Fold the head on the line. Glue the head to one end the body, attaching each side of the head to a side of the body. Repeat with the tail, gluing it to the other end of the body.

4. Glue the legs to the body, as shown on page 98, then fold along the lines to create feet.

5. Stand the alligator on a flat surface.

★ ALLIGATOR PAGE FRAMER

Encourage students to write short stories, skits, poems, songs, or other text about alligators. Or, have them draw imaginative pictures or cartoons of these creatures. When finished, distribute photocopies of the alligator patterns on pages 99–100. To make a page framer, ask students to color and cut out the patterns and glue them to the edges of a sheet of construction paper, as shown on page 100. Then have them attach their written work or drawing to the front of the page framer.

★ GROWING 'GATOR

To make a growing alligator, distribute the patterns on page 101 to each student. Also, provide a long strip of paper that's about 3 ½ inches wide at one end and 2 ½ inches wide at the other end. Have students color and cut out their alligator patterns, then glue the head to the wide end of their paper strip and the tail to the narrow end. (The paper strip will be the alligator's body.) Next, help students accordion-fold the body, making the sections as wide as desired. After preparing their 'gator, invite students to fill in the sections of its body with alligator-related facts, vocabulary words, rhymes, and so on. To make their 'gator grow or shrink, students simply unfold or fold its body.

★ ALLIGATOR HEADBAND

Invite students to make these cute headbands to wear during their alligator-related activities. To begin, students cut out a tagboard photocopy of the visor pattern (page 102). Then they fold down the teeth and fold up the snout. Next, students glue the top part of the alligator head to a two-inch wide strip of green construction paper (about 24 inches long). Finally, they fit the strip around their head, staple the ends together, and trim off any excess.

Amphibian or Reptile?

The name of my animal is _____

It is: ☐ an amphibian   ☐ a reptile

It can be found _____

_____

My animal eats _____

_____

Some interesting facts about
my animal are

_____

_____

_____

_____

_____

_____

This is a drawing of my animal.

June Monthly Idea Book © Scholastic Teaching Resources

June Monthly Idea Book © Scholastic Teaching Resources

Frogs and toads may look alike, but frogs have smooth, soft skin. Toads have rough, bumpy skin.

1

Frogs and toads are amphibians. This means they live both on land and in the water.

2

The mother frog lays her eggs near vegetation in a pond of water.

3

Tiny tadpoles hatch from the eggs. The tadpoles breathe through gills and feed on plants in the water.

4

Tadpoles are fast swimmers. They propel themselves through water with their fish-like tails.

5

Soon the tadpoles begin to change. They grow small legs on the back of their bodies. Then front legs begin to appear.

6

As tadpoles grow, their tails get shorter. Their front and back legs develop and get bigger. At last the tadpoles look like small frogs.

7

As it grows more, a frog spends some of its time on land. There, it catches its main source of food— insects!

8

Leaping Frogs

START

5.

6.

7.

8.

9.

10.

12.

11.

24.

21.

23.

22.

25.

FINISH

Frog

Spring

There are many kinds of turtles, but all turtles have shells. Their shells make these animals unique and different from other reptiles.

1

Some turtles live in water and some live on land. Land turtles are often called tortoises. Turtles can live to be a hundred years old and may grow to more than one thousand pounds.

2

Most water turtles are meat eaters. They feed on small fish. Land turtles are vegetarians and eat only plants.

3

A turtle's shell is made of bone that helps protect its body and vital organs. Some turtles, like a box turtle, can pull its head, legs, and tail into its shell to protect itself.

4

June Monthly Idea Book © Scholastic Teaching Resources

At times, a box turtle might get turned upside down. When this happens, the turtle has a very hard time turning itself back over.

5

All turtles lay their eggs on land. The mother digs a hole in soft dirt or sand. The she lays her eggs in the hole and covers them with dirt.

6

The mother turtle leaves her nest of eggs and never returns. She does not care for the eggs or baby turtles once they hatch.

7

In about three months, the hatchlings break through the tough shells of their eggs. Then the baby turtles set out on their own to find food and water.

8

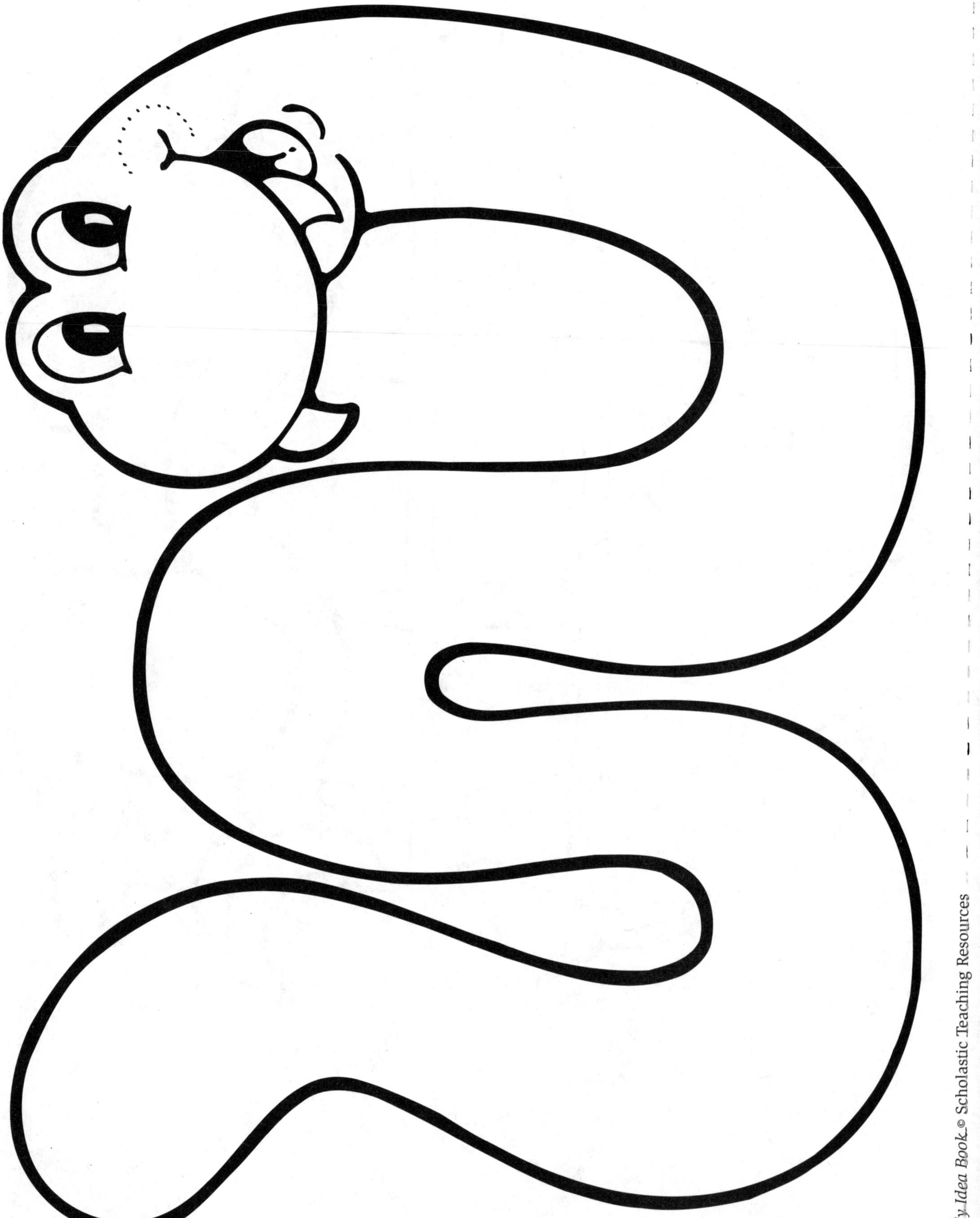

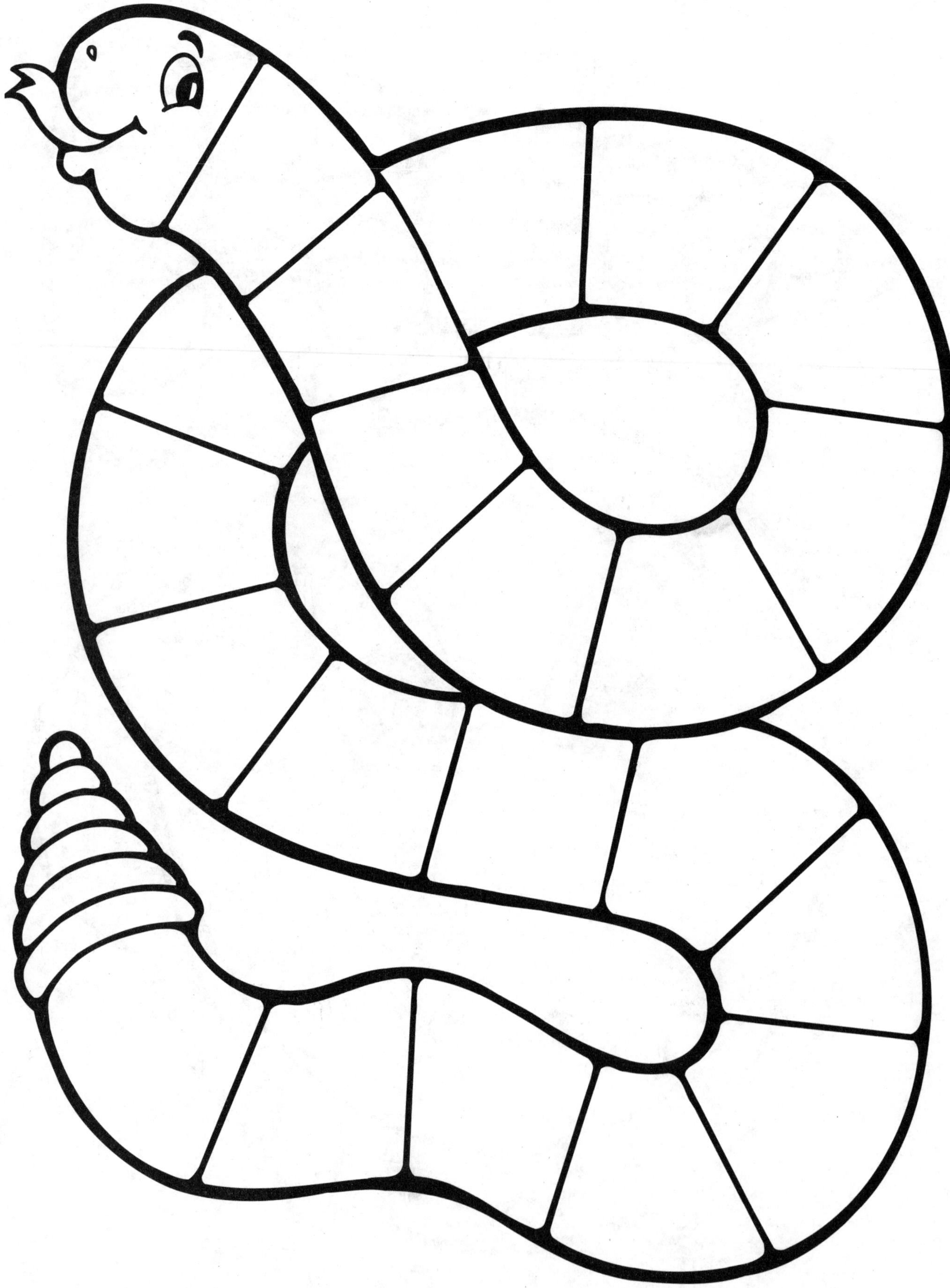

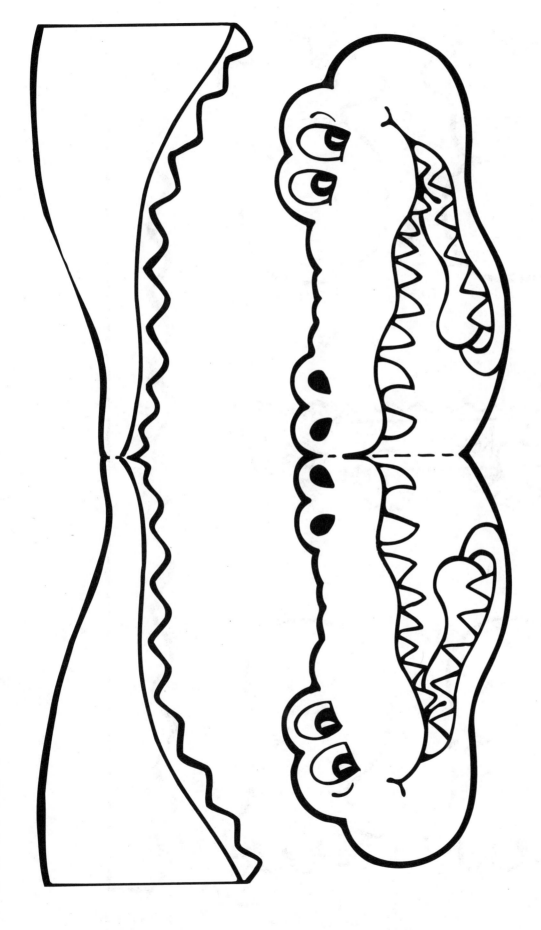

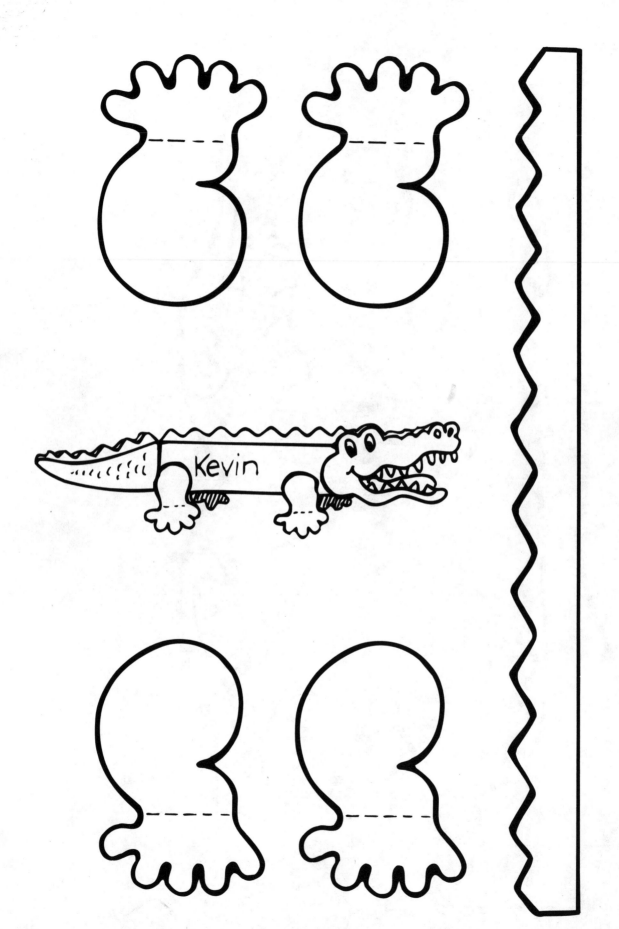

Kevin

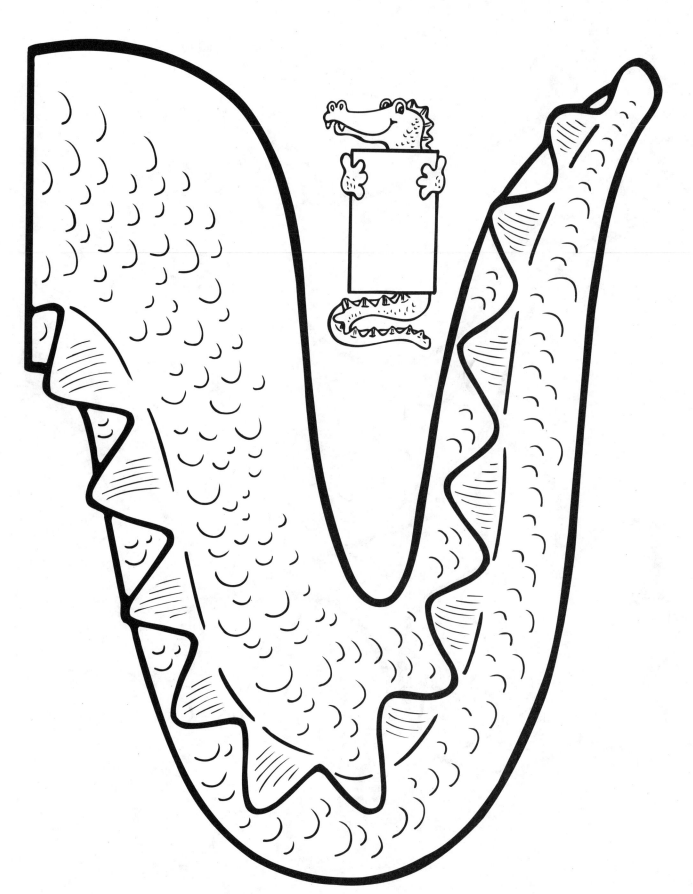

June Monthly Idea Book © Scholastic Teaching Resources

UNDER THE SEA

Millions of different kinds of animals live in the sea. In fact, the ocean, which covers about three quarters of the earth's surface, is the world's largest habitat. The waters of the ocean are divided into three zones: the sunlight zone, the twilight zone, and the midnight zone. Ocean dwellers might live in only one zone, or they might move into and out of two or even all three of the zones. As students learn about intriguing sea animals—such as a variety of fish, sharks, whales, octopuses, crabs, starfish, and seahorses—encourage them to share interesting facts and other information about their discoveries.

Suggested Activities

★ SEA ANIMAL REPORT

Inspire some science-based inquiry into ocean life with this activity. First, explain that students will choose a sea animal to research, using the Internet, nonfiction books, videos, documentaries, and perhaps interviews with specialists at a local aquarium. Distribute photocopies of page 110 for students to fill out as they discover facts and other interesting information about their animal. (If they need more space to write, they can use the back of the page.) After students complete their reports, invite them to share their findings with the class. If desired, collect the pages and bind them together to create a class book about sea animals.

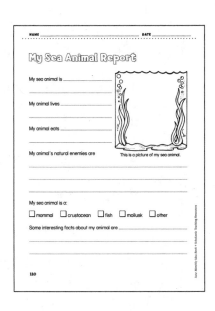

★ FISH FACTS

The ocean is home to a vast variety of fish. Work with students to create a list of saltwater fish, such as angelfish, butterfly fish, clownfish, lionfish, pufferfish, salmon, and tuna. Then have them choose a fish from the list and do research to learn about its characteristics, habits, survival skills, and so on. Distribute photocopies of the fish stationery on page 111 for students to use when they are ready to write the final draft of their findings. Invite students to share their written work with the class. If desired, display the pages on a bulletin board titled "Fantastic Fish!"

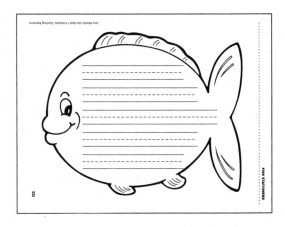

FISH PAPER-BAG PUPPET

Invite students to make puppets to use when they present their fish findings from "Fish Facts" (page 103). To begin, distribute a small paper bag and a photocopy of the patterns on page 112 to each student. Ask students to color and cut out the patterns. Then have them glue the fish's head to the bottom flap of the bag and its body to the front of the bag below the flap. If desired, invite students to use craft items, such as glitter glue or sequins, to add embellishments to their puppets.

FISH FLASH CARDS

Reinforce the skills your students are learning with flash cards that fit the theme of this unit. Simply photocopy the cards on page 113 and cut them out. You can program the cutouts for use as flash cards to teach:

- letters and numbers

- math facts

- content-area vocabulary words

- sight words

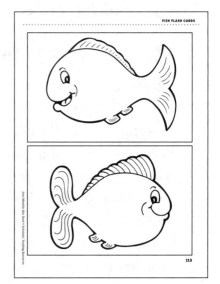

The cards are ideal for learning-center activities, but you might also use them to create a magnetic fishing game, label job charts, group students, and more. To store, just put them in a resealable plastic bag.

AMAZING SHARKS

Toothy sharks often captivate the interest and imagination of children. Have students do research to discover and learn about different kinds of sharks that live in the ocean. If desired, make a list of shark names. Then ask students to choose a shark from the list to research and write about. To make a page framer for their written work, distribute copies of the shark patterns on page 114. Have students color and cut out the patterns. Then instruct them to glue their shark's head and tail to the top and bottom of a sheet of construction paper and the fins to the left and right sides of the page.

Finally, have students attach their writing to the page framer and display on a bulletin board.

To extend the learning, distribute photocopies of the shark patterns on page 115. Have students cut out the patterns, then write shark facts on the cutouts. Add the fact sharks to the bulletin board.

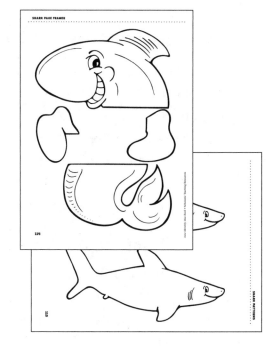

★ WONDERFUL WHALES

Introduce the topic of whales by explaining that these large sea animals are mammals, not fish. Review the common characteristics of all whales. Then create a list of different kinds of whales, including orcas, baleen whales, belugas, blue whales, sperm whales, and humpback whales. Ask students to choose a whale from the list to research. As they search nonfiction books, the Internet, and other sources for information, encourage them to consider these questions:

- ■ How do whales swim?

- ■ Can whales hear or smell?

- ■ Do whales have teeth?

- ■ What do whales eat?

- ■ Why do whales have blowholes?

- ■ How long can a whale hold its breath?

- ■ What is the name for a baby whale?

- ■ How do whales communicate with each other?

- ■ Do whales migrate? If so, why?

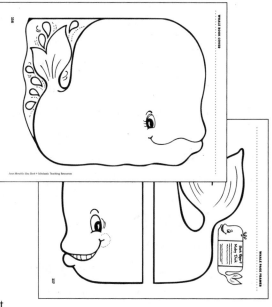

After completing their research, have students write about their findings. Invite them to use the pattern on page 116 to create a cover for their written work, then add a title and name line to their cover. Or, students might create a page framer for their work. To make, they color and cut out the whale patterns on page 117, then glue the cutouts to the sides of a sheet of construction paper. When done, students can attach their work to the page framer and display on a bulletin board.

THE AWESOME OCTOPUS

The octopus got its name from a Greek word meaning "eight-footed." Ask students if they have ever seen an octopus. Invite them to share their observations as well as other information they know about these boneless animals. Afterward, have them do research to learn more. Students can write about their findings, then make one or more of the following projects to use when presenting their written work to the class.

Octopus Paper-Bag Puppet

Distribute small paper bags and photocopies of the patterns on page 118 to students. Have them color and cut out the patterns. Then instruct students to glue their octopus's head to the bottom flap of the bag and its mouth and body to the front of the bag below the flap. If desired, students can glue on inverted sequins to add texture to the suckers on their octopus's tentacles.

Curly-Legged Octopus

For this easy-to-make octopus, give each student two photocopies of the octopus pattern on page 119. (You might copy the patterns onto colored sheets of construction paper.) Have students cut out their patterns, then glue the top part of their cutouts together back-to-back, leaving the bottom open and the tentacles free. Next, help students curl each tentacle around a pencil. Finally, have them stand their octopuses upright on a flat surface.

Hinged Octopus

Prepare one photocopy of page 120 and two of page 121 for each student. Distribute the pages and have students color and cut out the octopus patterns. Then ask them to punch a hole in the bottom of their octopus's body and in each arm where indicated. To assemble, students stack the eight arms, lining up the holes. Then they use a brass fastener to attach the stacked arms to the body, as shown on page 120. If desired, invite students to glue a wide craft stick to the back of their octopus to use as a handle. They can move their octopus in a variety of ways to make it dance or to spin and wiggle its arms in amusing ways.

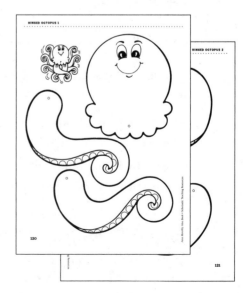

June Monthly Idea Book © Scholastic Teaching Resources

★ PAPER-PLATE CRAB

As students make these projects, point out the different parts of a crab. Afterward, have students do research to learn more about these odd-looking, leggy creatures. They can write crab facts on plain index cards to display with their crabs. To prepare, distribute photocopies the crab patterns (pages 122 and 123) and a paper plate to each student. Then instruct students to do the following to make their crab:

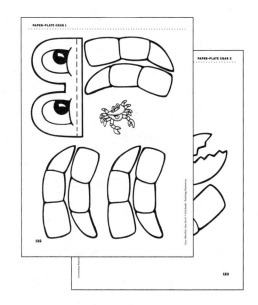

1. Color (or paint) the paper plate. This will be the crab's body. Fold the body in half. (The opening will serve as a mouth.)

2. Color and cut out all of the patterns.

3. Fold back the tab on the eyes cutout. Glue the tab to the top of the body, as shown on page 122.

4. Glue a claw and four smaller legs to each side of the body.

★ STARFISH FACT GARLAND

Starfish can be found in a variety of colors, shapes, and sizes. However, they all have a star-like shape. Work with students to discover facts about starfish to list on chart paper. Then invite students to color and cut out several copies of the starfish pattern on page 124. Ask them to write a different starfish fact on the back of each cutout. To make a garland, have students glue their starfish together, connecting them by gluing the end of one starfish's arm to the arm of the next starfish. To complete, help students attach a length of yarn to each side of their starfish garland. Hang the garlands on a clothesline or suspend them across a bulletin board or window.

★ SEAHORSE STICK PUPPETS

Have students do research and write about the unique and easily recognizable seahorse. Then invite them to make stick puppets to use when they present their findings. Simply have students color and cut out the seahorse patterns on page 125, then add a craft-stick handle to complete their puppet.

★ PAPER-PLATE JELLYFISH

Jellyfish are fascinating creatures. Invite students to share what they know about jellyfish. Then work with them to learn more about these multi-tentacled invertebrates. Have students write different jellyfish facts on plain index cards. Next, invite them to create paper-plate jellyfish to display with their fact cards. To make, have students color or paint a small paper plate, then add ribbon tentacles and a yarn hanger to the plate, as shown. To display, help students hang their jellyfish on a bulletin board and attach their fact cards to the spaces between and around the jellyfish.

★ UNDER-THE-SEA BINGO

Reinforce sea-animal-related vocabulary words with a game of Bingo! To prepare, make several photocopies of the game board on page 126 and a single copy of the game cards on pages 127–128. On each game board, fill in the boxes with the names of different sea animals that appear on the game cards. (Use a different combination of names on each game board.) Copy the programmed game boards, making enough for each student in a group (or the whole class) to have one. Then cut out the game cards and laminate all of the game pieces. Supply players with Bingo chips or dried beans to use as markers. To play, follow the rules for a traditional game of Bingo.

★ WHALE SKILLS WHEEL

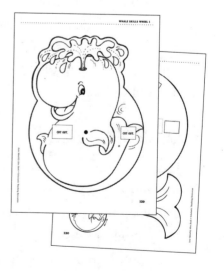

Use the whale wheel patterns on pages 129–130 to reinforce math skills and more. To prepare, write a problem in each of the large boxes (outlined in gray). Write the answer in the small box directly opposite each problem on the right. Cut out the whale, tail, and wheel. Then carefully cut out the "windows" on the whale. Use one brass fastener to attach the wheel to the whale and another to attach the tail, as shown on page 130. To use, students turn to the wheel so that a problem appears in the left window. They solve the problem and then slide the tail away from the right window to check their answer.

★ UNDER-THE-SEA MOBILE

Invite students to construct these easy-to-make mobiles to display or use as a prop when sharing their sea-animal knowledge. First, give each student a photocopy of the mobile patterns (pages 131–133), two 1-foot lengths of yarn, and scissors. Also provide glue, a hole punch, and an assortment of craft items, such as glitter, sequins, colored cotton balls, and tissue-paper scraps. Then have students do the following to make their mobile:

1. Cut out the starfish and other sea animal patterns.

2. On the back of each cutout, write a fact or something interesting about the animal pictured on the front of that piece.

3. Color or decorate the front of each piece. (If desired, use craft items to add texture and interest.)

4. Punch four holes in the starfish and one hole near the top of each of the other sea animals where indicated.

5. Cut one of the 1-foot lengths of yarn into three pieces of varying lengths. Tie a length of yarn to the hole in the fish, octopus, and crab. Tie the other end to a hole at the bottom of the starfish, as shown.

6. To make a hanger, tie the other 1-foot length of yarn to the hole at the top of the starfish.

★ SEA-ANIMAL CORNER PAGE TOPPERS

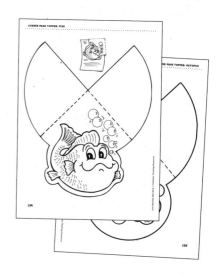

Students can make these page toppers to use as bookmarks for the sea-animal books they are reading. Distribute tape and photocopies of pages 134 and 135. Ask students to choose a pattern and do the following to make a bookmark:

1. Color and cut out the pattern.

2. Fold back the two sides of the cutout where indicated, bringing the straight edges together at the back of the bookmark. Use tape to secure.

3. Slip the bookmark over the top corner of a book to mark the last page read or pages of interest.

My Sea Animal Report

My sea animal is _____

_____

My animal lives _____

_____

My animal eats _____

_____

My animal's natural enemies are

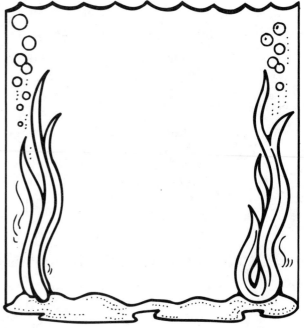

This is a picture of my sea animal.

_____

_____

_____

My sea animal is a:

☐ mammal   ☐ crustacean   ☐ fish   ☐ mollusk   ☐ other

Some interesting facts about my animal are _____

_____

_____

June Monthly Idea Book © Scholastic Teaching Resources.

June Monthly Idea Book © Scholastic Teaching Resources

June Monthly Idea Book © Scholastic Teaching Resources

June Monthly Idea Book © Scholastic Teaching Resources

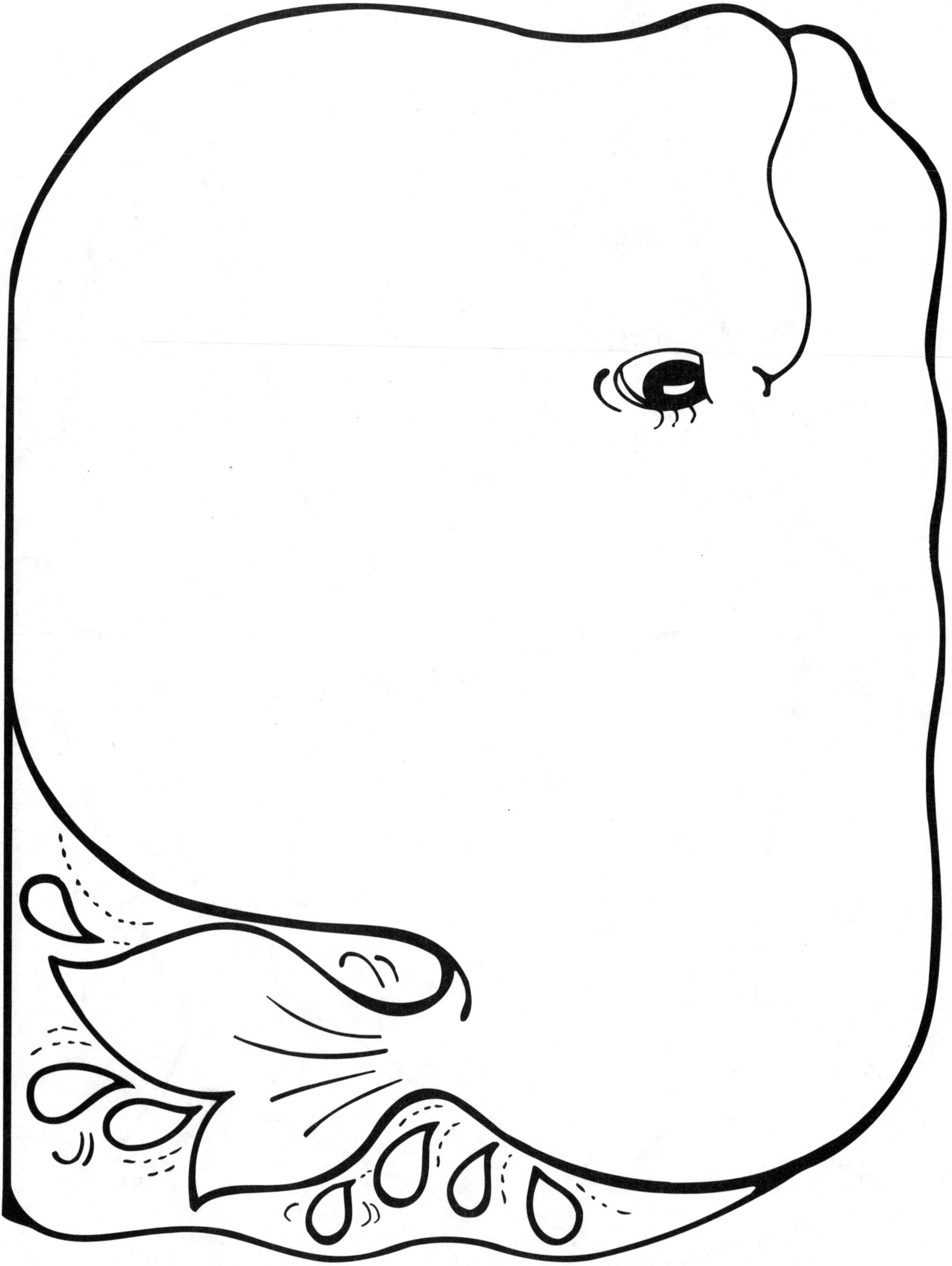

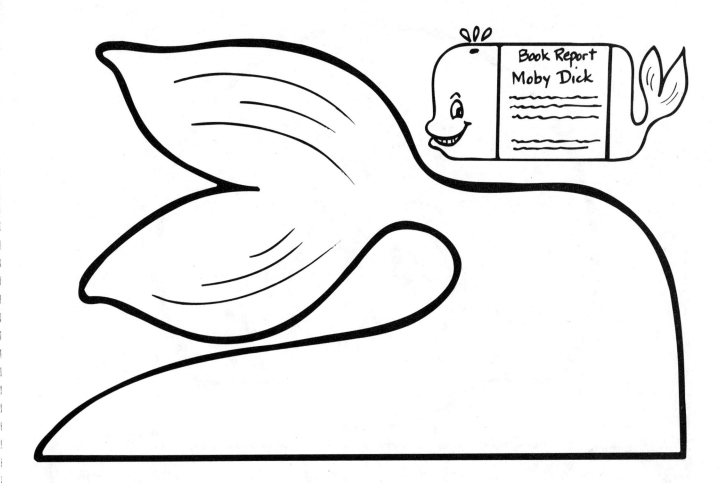

Book Report
Moby Dick

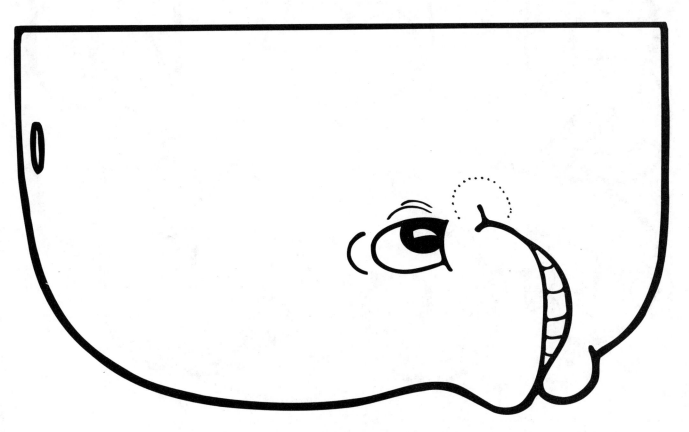

June Monthly Idea Book © Scholastic Teaching Resources

June Monthly Idea Book © Scholastic Teaching Resources

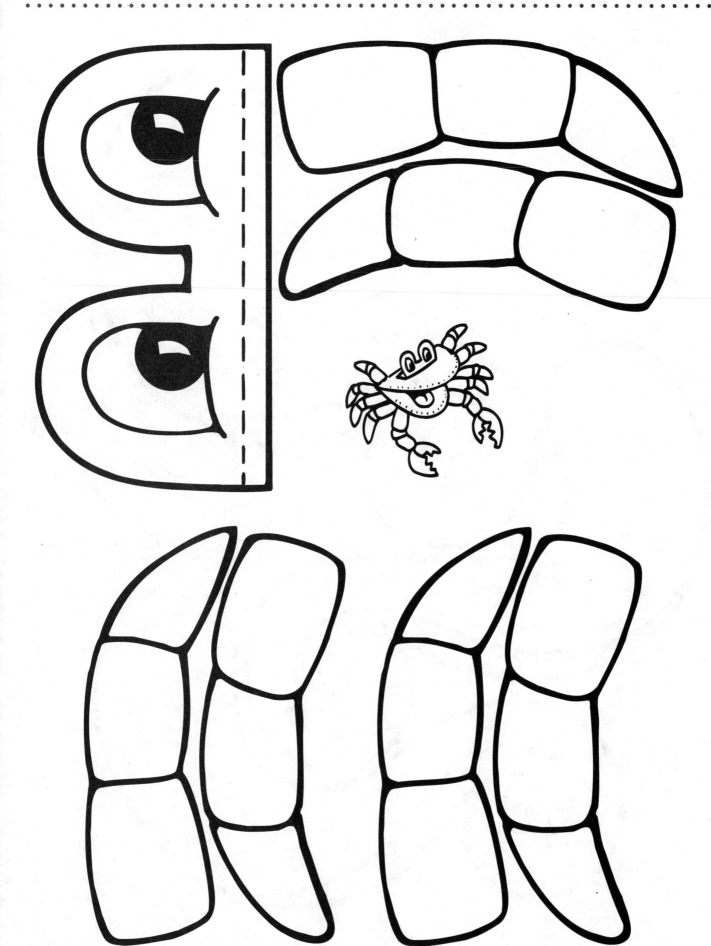

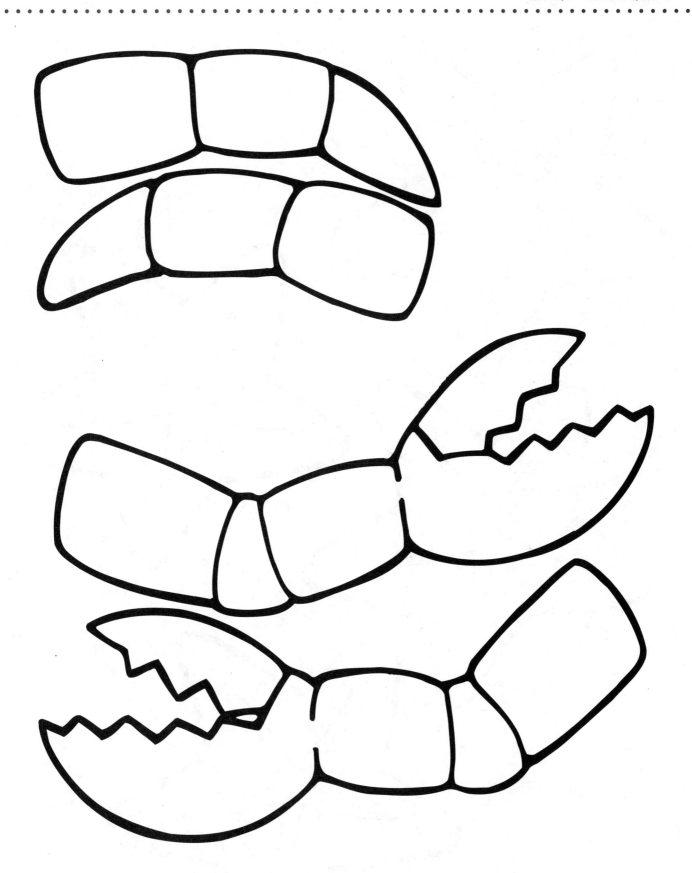

Under-the-Sea
BINGO

FREE

barracuda	crab	halibut	jellyfish
blue marlin	dolphin	hammerhead shark	killer whale
beluga whale	eel	herring	lobster
clam	flounder	humpback whale	manta ray
clownfish	great white shark	lionfish	mussel

octopus	sardine	seahorse	starfish
oyster	sea anemone	seal	sunfish
porpoise	sea otter	shrimp	swordfish
sailfish	sea turtle	sponge	tiger shark
salmon	sea urchin	squid	tuna

June Monthly Idea Book © Scholastic Teaching Resources

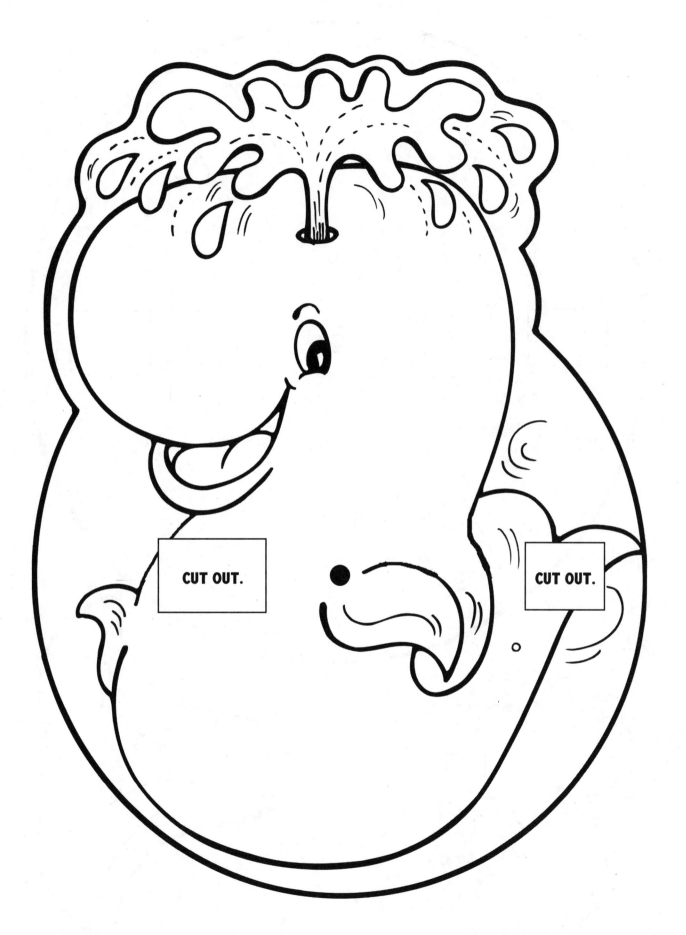

CUT OUT.

CUT OUT.

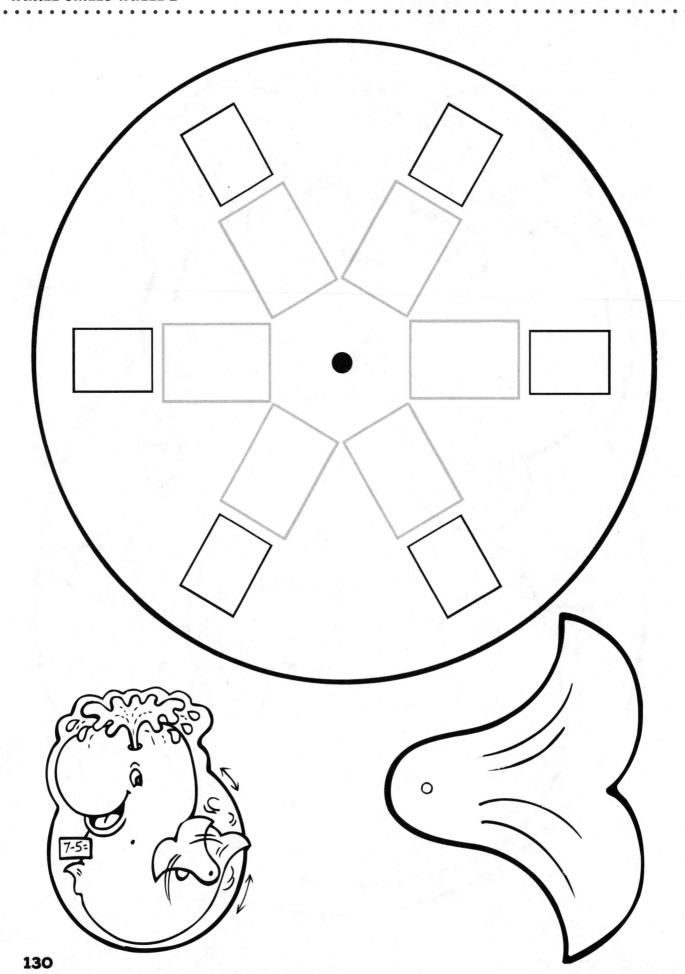

June Monthly Idea Book © Scholastic Teaching Resources

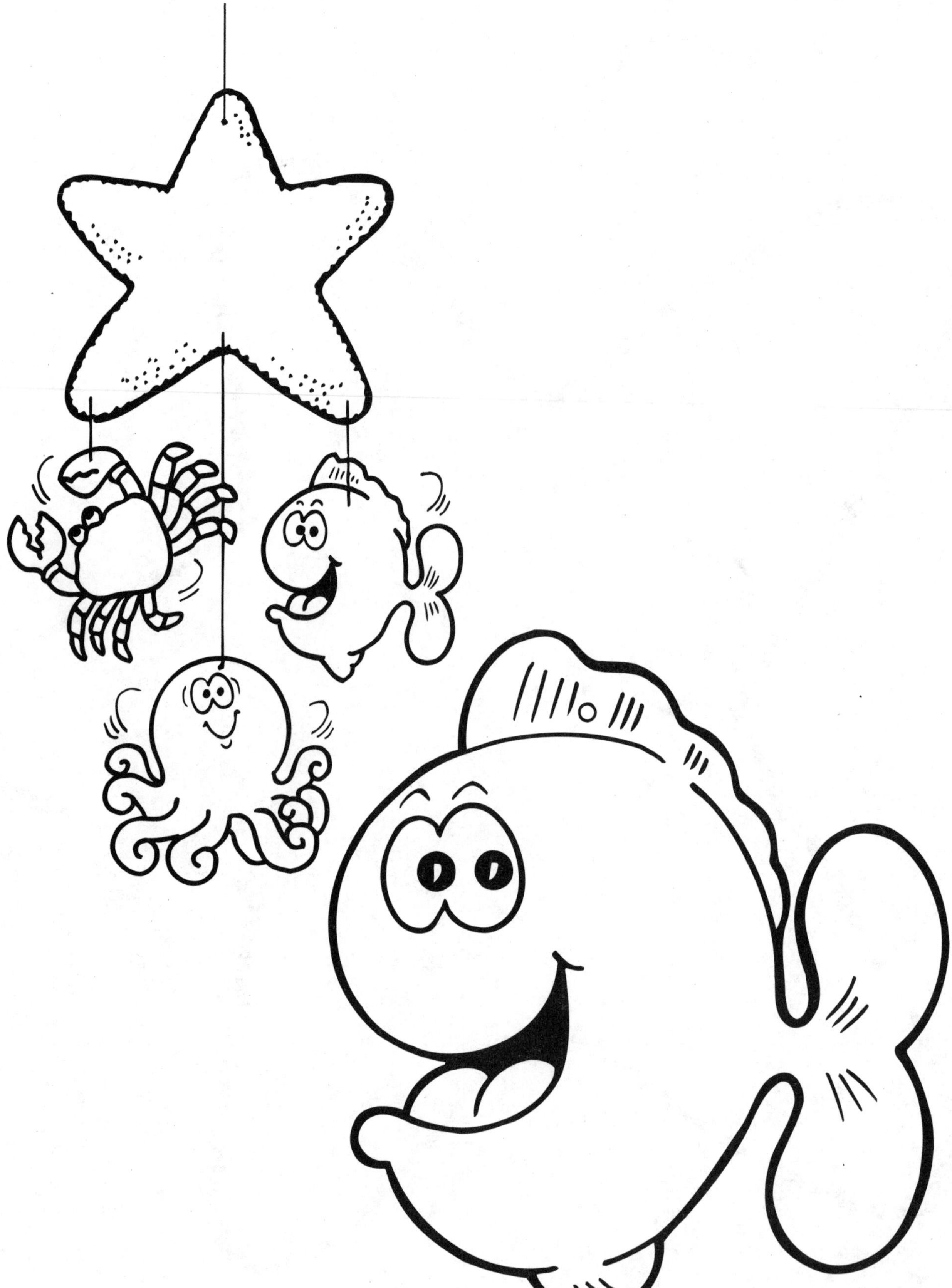

AWARDS, INCENTIVES, AND MORE

Getting Started

Make several photocopies of the reproducibles on pages 138 through 142. Giving out the bookmarks, pencil toppers, notes, and certificates will show students your enthusiasm for their efforts and achievements. Plus, bookmarks and pencil toppers are a fun treat for students celebrating birthdays.

- Provide materials for decorating, including markers, color pencils, and stickers.

- Encourage students to bring home their creations to share and celebrate with family members.

★ BOOKMARKS

1. Photocopy onto tagboard and cut apart.

2. For more fanfare, punch a hole on one end and tie on a length of colorful ribbon or yarn.

★ PENCIL TOPPERS

1. Photocopy onto tagboard and cut out.

2. Use an art knife to cut through the Xs.

3. Slide a pencil through the Xs as shown.

★ SEND-HOME NOTES

1. Photocopy and cut apart.

2. Record the child's name and the date.

3. Add your signature.

4. Add more details about the student's day on the back of the note.

★ CERTIFICATES

1. Photocopy.

2. Record the child's name and other information, as directed.

3. Add details about the child's achievement (if applicable), then add your signature and the date.

FOR A "WHALE" OF A GOOD TIME...
READ A BOOK!

Take a dive into reading!

Leap into a good book!

_____
Student's Name

took a bite out of learning today!

_____   _____
Teacher   Date

_____
Student's Name

flew high today!

_____   _____
Teacher   Date

_____
Student's Name

caught a lot of praise today!

_____   _____
Teacher   Date

_____
Student's Name

was a star student today!

_____   _____
Teacher   Date

June Monthly Idea Book © Scholastic Teaching Resources

Student of the Week

Name _____

School _____

Date _____

Teacher _____

Certificate of Achievement

presented to

_____

Name

in recognition of

_____

_____

_____

_____

Date

_____

Teacher

June Monthly Idea Book © Scholastic Teaching Resources